DEVELOPING

A Character Education Program

ONE SCHOOL DISTRICT'S EXPERIENCE

HENRY A. HUFFMAN

Association for Supervision and Curriculum Development

The Character Education Partnership

Association for Supervision and Curriculum Development
1250 N. Pitt Street, Alexandria, VA 22314
Telephone (703) 549-9110, Fax (703) 549-3891

The Character Education Partnership
1250 N. Pitt Street, Alexandria, VA 22314
Telephone (703) 739-9515, Fax (703) 739-4967

About the Author

Henry A. Huffman is Assistant Superintendent for Instruction in the Mt. Lebanon School District, Pittsburgh, Pennsylvania. In January 1995, he will leave Mt. Lebanon to work full-time in the field of character education. He can be reached at his home address; 412 Mary Lane, Canonsburg, PA 15317, or by phone at (412) 745-4625.

ASCD publications present a variety of viewpoints. The views expressed or implied in this publication should not be interpreted as official positions of the Association.

Printed in the United States of America.

Ronald S. Brandt, *Executive Editor*
Nancy Modrak, *Managing Editor, ASCD Books*
Julie Houtz, *Senior Associate Editor*
Sydney Petty, *Copy Editor*
Gary Bloom, *Manager, Design and Production Services*
Stephanie Justen, *Assistant Manager, Design and Production Services*
Valerie Sprague, *Desktop Publisher*

ASCD Stock No.: 1-94225
Price: $13.95
ISBN: 0-87120-236-0

Library of Congress Cataloging-in-Publication Data

Huffman, Henry A.
　　　Developing a character education program : one school district's experience / Henry A. Huffman.
　　　　　p.　　cm.
　　　Includes bibliographical references.
　　　ISBN 0-87120-236-0 (pbk.)
　　　1. Moral education—Pennsylvania—Mt. Lebanon School District (Mount Lebanon)—Case studies.　I. Title.
　　LC 311.H84　1994
　　370.11'4'097419—dc20　　(2) Values education
　　　　　　　　　　　　　　　　　　　　　　　　　94-36454
　　　　　　　　　　　　　　　　　　　　　　　　　CIP

Developing a Character Education Program
One School District's Experience

Acknowledgments

I want to express my deep gratitude to Tom Lickona for his careful reading of this manuscript and his invaluable suggestions. I am grateful for his continuing contributions to my education as a character educator. I have also been fortunate to work in a community that has supported our character education initiative. To my Mt. Lebanon colleagues, many thanks for your commitment to this important undertaking. Finally, to my wife, Betty Jane, and my sons, Jason and Nathan, please continue to help me learn to integrate knowledge of the head, heart, and hand.

Foreword

Tom Lickona

There are at least three compelling reasons for schools to provide character education. The first is that we need good character to be fully human. We need strengths of mind, heart, and will—qualities like good judgment, honesty, empathy, caring, persistence, and self-discipline—to be capable of work and love, two of the hallmarks of human maturity.

A second reason to make character education a high priority is that schools are better places—certainly more conducive to teaching and learning—when they are civil and caring communities that promulgate, teach, celebrate, and enforce the values on which good character is based.

A third reason for character education is that it is essential to the task of building a moral society. It is painfully clear that our contemporary society suffers severe social and moral problems: the breakdown of the family, rampant greed at a time when one of every four children lives in poverty, dishonesty at all levels of society, a rising tide of sleaze in the media, the deterioration of civility in everyday life, the breakdown of sexual morality, widespread drug and alcohol abuse, physical and sexual abuse of children, an epidemic of violence, and the devaluation of human life represented by a million and a half abortions each year. And, as is typically the case, society's problems are most visibly reflected in its youth. Ten troubling youth trends[1] indicate the dimensions of our difficulty:

1. Rising youth violence
2. Increasing dishonesty (lying, cheating, and stealing)

---

[1]For documentation of these trends, see *The Ethics of American Youth: A Warning and a Call to Action* (Marina del Ray, Calif.: Josephson Institute of Ethics, 1990); T. Lickona, *Educating for Character* (New York: Bantam Books, 1991); and W. Kilpatrick, *Why Johnny Can't Tell Right from Wrong* (New York: Simon and Schuster, 1992).

3. Greater disrespect for parents, teachers, and other legitimate authority figures
4. Increasing peer cruelty
5. A rise in bigotry and hate crime
6. The deterioration of language
7. A decline in the work ethic
8. Increasing self-centeredness, accompanied by declining personal and civic responsibility
9. A surge of self-destructive behaviors such as premature sexual activity, substance abuse, and suicide
10. Growing ethical illiteracy, including ignorance of moral knowledge as basic as the Golden Rule and the tendency to engage in behaviors injurious to self or others without thinking it wrong.

In response to these moral danger signs, interest in character education is steadily building. Two national organizations, the Character Education Partnership and the Character Counts Coalition, have formed within the past two years to promote character education nationwide. A spate of recent books[2] advocate character education as our best hope for addressing a wide range of student academic and behavior problems. At this writing, Congress is drafting legislation that would fund state and school district activity to develop character education materials and teacher education programs aimed at teaching "core ethical values" such as respect, responsibility, trustworthiness, fairness, and caring. Private foundations are seeking character education efforts to support. Summer 1994 saw the first White House Conference on Character-Building for a Democratic and Civil Society.

In this fertile context, Henry Huffman's *Developing a Character Education Program: One School District's Experience* is a timely and much-needed contribution. He offers a comprehensive concept of character, what he calls "a morality of the head, the heart, and the

---

[2] W. Kilpatrick's *Why Johnny Can't Tell Right from Wrong* (New York: Simon and Schuster, 1992); J. Benniga's *Moral, Character, and Civic Education in the Elementary School* (New York: Teachers College Press, 1991); T. Lickona's *Educating for Character* (New York: Bantam Books, 1991); and Wynne and Ryan's *Reclaiming Our Schools: A Handbook for Teaching Character, Academics, and Discipline* (New York: Merrill, 1992).

hand." He describes an all-embracing approach to character education, one that pays scrupulous attention to the moral impact of everything a school district does and one that sees school board members, administrators, faculty, classified staff, parents, and students as all having key roles in developing a districtwide ethos that supports the core ethical values at every opportunity.

The distinctive value of this cogent, lucid monograph is that it addresses the nuts-and-bolts questions most on the minds of school practitioners: How to get character education started? How to get consensus about the core values? How to get all the relevant constituencies on board and keep everyone informed? How to keep controversies about matters such as outcome-based education from sabotaging the character effort? What is the proper role of religion in a public school character education program? How to help teachers and other staff develop the needed understandings and skills? How to offset the negative value influences of sex, violence, and materialism in the media? How to involve parents and respect parents' right to know about, and consent to, what the school is doing in the area of values and character? How to handle the sensitive question of evaluation—both program evaluation and the evaluation of the character-related behaviors of individual students?

Huffman answers these questions chiefly by telling the story of his own district's ongoing character education effort in Mt. Lebanon, Pennsylvania, and by drawing "lessons learned" from that experience. He speaks with special credibility because he has been the hands-on leader of his district's effort. As assistant superintendent, he chaired the overall Character Development Strategy Team as well as three of the Implementation Teams charged with developing detailed action plans. He spoke often to PTAs and civic groups, observed and taught the literature-based Heartwood Ethics Curriculum, and took part in staff development. This in-the-trenches experience enables him to report with authority and humility on what worked and where mistakes of commission and omission were made. I know of no other resource in the character education literature that provides such a rich picture of a district's planning and implementation process.

If there is a single principle underlying the comprehensive approach recommended by Huffman, it is this: Good character comes from living in moral communities, communities of character in which virtue is modeled, taught, and affirmed. In order to foster good character, the school—indeed, Huffman emphasizes, *the whole district*—must have a strong positive ethos. Incongruence between a district's core values and its operation, Huffman warns, can quickly undermine the integrity and effectiveness of a character education initiative. Potentially difficult matters, such as how a district responds to its critics and how it handles labor-management negotiations, must be viewed as tests of its commitment to the core values.

The greatest danger facing the character education movement, educational researchers Cheryl and David Aspy observe, is that severe social and moral problems will be met with superficial and weak educational efforts. When weak efforts inevitably fail to ameliorate the problems, people will become discouraged and say, "We tried character education, and it failed." I strongly recommend this book to any school district that is serious about character education, if it wants to maximize the likelihood that schools—working with parents, churches, business, and community agencies—will make a positive difference in the character of the young and, eventually, in our society.

Introduction

Although I enjoy my work as a school administrator, my first professional love is teaching. I indulge this passion by teaching part-time at two local universities and serving as a guest teacher in my school system. Several years ago, I was discussing Jane Austen's *Pride and Prejudice* with the students in a 12th grade Advanced Placement English class when a young woman suddenly blurted, "How *could* they?" When I asked her what she meant, she said she couldn't understand how middle-class women could have tolerated such empty lives, consumed with gossip and discussions of potential husbands, extravagant balls, and afternoon teas.

One of the things I enjoy about teaching is what it contributes to my own learning. As this young woman spoke, a light bulb went on in my mind, and I decided to pose a question to the class. I said we look with disdain at the lives of late 18th century women, we study with disbelief the practice of selling human beings as property in this country in the mid 19th century, and we lament the sexism that denied women the right to vote earlier in this century. We can make those observations from a late 20th century perspective that we regard as enlightened and possibly morally superior to earlier periods. "However," I asked the class, "what is there about the current period that will prompt people a hundred years from now to inquire, 'How could they have tolerated that?'"

The class cited several good possibilities: drugs, the environment, the values implicit in the astronomical salaries of entertainers and athletes. My contribution to this list was our society's treatment of children. Recent social developments have put our youngsters at great risk. I discussed the observations of Neil Postman in *The Disappearance of Childhood* and David Elkind in *The Hurried Child*. Postman (1982) views childhood as a concept developed during the Renaissance and now threatened by forces such as the electronic media that "find it impossible to withhold any secrets. Without secrets, of course, there can be no such thing as childhood" (p. 80). Elkind (1981) sees similar forces at work: "We hurry children because stress induces us to put our own needs ahead of their needs" (p. 28).

My point about childhood grew out of a concern I had developed a few years earlier. In 1988, as I concluded a presentation of budget proposals for instructional change to our school board, a member of the board asked what items I might have included if we had more time or money to spend. I answered that as a parent and educator, I felt we should begin talking about what role schools should play in character education. Certain social trends (the growing mass media influence, changes in the family, increases in violent crime among our youth) were forcing me to ponder the future of our country, especially if we didn't begin to change their direction.

Articles on character education were just beginning to appear in the professional journals and popular press, and they soon provided the reinforcing documentation that I needed. Later that year, I attended an international conference on moral education where I participated in a workshop conducted by Tom Lickona, author of *Raising Good Children* and *Educating for Character*. He helped me begin to understand the moral development of human beings and the role that caregivers, educators, and parents must play in that process.

That year I decided I had a responsibility as assistant superintendent for instruction to ask what role our schools should play in educating for character. That decision marked the beginning of the professional and personal journey I have described in this book.

My work in character education relates to an aspect of public education that has disturbed me throughout much of my career: the transactional or reactive nature of our leadership role. Ideally, we should, and often do, work with our constituents to develop goals and then enter into an agreement (transactional leadership) to lead them in those directions. Too often, however, our goals are quickly formulated as reactions (reactive leadership) to some problem or crisis. All too rarely do we manifest what Burns (1978) calls transformational leadership. We fail to transform our constituents' vision of the possible or desirable into something larger, more altruistic.

This book challenges educators to provide transformational leadership in character education. In those communities where people are not aware of the growing national movement to have schools return to their historical mission of educating for character, I urge my colleagues to make a case for character education.

Whether you become involved in the movement now, as a result of a "transformational" initiative, or later, as the result of some "transaction" growing out of external pressure or a mandate, I hope your efforts will not be limited to the schools. As I have discovered through my character education journey, I need to grow as a parent responsible for the moral development of our two sons. But I have also come to realize that I must address the character education needs of this nation from my role as citizen, member of a religious institution, neighbor, and consumer. We must seek to influence policy in all sectors of our society. Schools alone will not alter the moral direction of this nation. Teachers and administrators who implement character education programs must use their knowledge and experience in assisting other institutions in their efforts to help students become ethical, responsible citizens.

I have spoken to many groups about the need to create character education partnerships, and I have been gratified to discover a public longing for concerted efforts to address the problems of crime and violence and the unethical behavior of politicians and other prominent people. I no longer spend much time presenting a social rationale for character education; the media have already made the case for me. Audiences are not so much interested in the *why* of character education as they are in the *how*.

Nevertheless, I have included the reasons for character education in this book because, even in the absence of challenges, educators need to be clear about why they are undertaking this effort. I hope that you detect passion in my words because for me, character education represents our highest calling and our most pressing need as educators. It is also a wonderful opportunity to exert a positive influence—an impulse that has attracted teachers to this profession for thousands of years.

I understand the call for higher academic standards, but I agree with Robert Coles, who observed during his 1993 ASCD keynote speech that Nazi Germany represented the highest literacy and educational levels then achieved in the Western world.

If we fail to reach new standards of character, our children will continue to be at great risk. And 100 hundred years from now some student may ask a teacher, "How could they have had so little regard for their children in the late 20th century?"

1

Getting Started

In 1988, as the assistant superintendent for instruction of the Mt. Lebanon School District, which lies just south of Pittsburgh, Pennsylvania, I decided that we needed to consider what role, if any, we should play in educating for character. How to get started was the first question.

I asked the president of our teachers' association and the president of the PTA Council what role the local schools needed to play to help students develop into ethical, responsible citizens. We decided to pursue that question by creating a study group of 10 teachers, administrators, and parents. We met for a year, investigating many aspects of character education. We defined terms, distinguishing among *character, ethics, morals, values,* and *social conventions.*

Although many people use these terms synonymously, we saw important differences. For example, we preferred to refer to *morals* as principles of right and wrong behavior and *ethics* as the application of moral principles to difficult questions of right or wrong, fairness, or equity. The important point is that individuals who are investigating character education in a particular setting reach agreement on how they will define the terms in their own school setting.

We studied schools of thought on character development and found educators who focused on behavior and others who were more concerned with moral reasoning. Integrative approaches that paid attention to both reasoning and behavior had the greatest appeal to us. Eventually, we found programs such as the Child Development Project of San Ramon, California (Murphy 1988), which were based on these integrative schools of thought.

Developing Support

We decided to increase staff and community awareness of the topic by bringing in a nationally recognized figure in the field of character education. We wanted a consultant who possessed first-hand knowledge of critical issues and actual programs and the ability to inspire a highly competent staff. Additionally, since the PTA planned to use the speaker for a parenting workshop, we wanted someone who had written for and consulted with parents.

The use of a consultant can facilitate or impede change efforts, depending on the fit between the district's needs and the consultant's style and background. We invited Tom Lickona, author of books and articles for parents and teachers, to spend two days in the district. He consulted with the study group, conducted a day-long voluntary workshop for staff who wanted to learn about character education, and presented an evening parenting program for the PTA. Approximately a third of the staff signed up for the workshop—a large response to a voluntary session for Mt. Lebanon. For the PTA program, more than 700 people paid $2 each to attend, a turnout unequaled in the PTA's history. Both responses revealed keen community and staff interest in the topic.

Following the workshop, I sent an invitation to all staff to participate in the study group. More than 40 teachers joined the group, which met after school on the teachers' own time. Four months after the initial Lickona workshop, the school board decided to map the district's future by writing a strategic plan. The decision to develop a strategic plan was totally unrelated to the study goup's work. The school board selected the strategic planning system developed by Bill Cook and retained the services of the Cambridge Group to direct the process. The district formed a Strategic Planning Team of 28 staff, residents, and students to write a five-year strategic plan, the period used in the Cook model. The effects of growing community and staff interest in character education were obvious in the mission statement:

> The mission of the Mt. Lebanon School District, as the leader of an educational partnership with the community, is to ensure that all students acquire the knowledge and skills to succeed and contribute as ethical, responsible citizens in a

rapidly changing global society through a challenging comprehensive program taught by an exceptional staff in a safe, caring environment.

The Strategic Planning Team developed nine strategies for achieving the mission statement. Three of the nine strategies were directly related to topics the Study Group had been discussing:

> Strategy 2—We will establish programs for the development and implementation of ethical and responsible student behavior.
>
> Strategy 3—We will create a caring environment that ensures the success of each student.
>
> Strategy 4—We will work with community groups to develop plans for students to have a variety of opportunities for involvement in community service.

The study group concluded that the selection of these three strategies, which were directly related to the scope of their investigations and the Lickona presentations to the staff and PTA, suggested strong community support for a character education initiative.

The acid test of that support occurred a year later when a political storm raged throughout the state over new curriculum regulations based on outcome-based education (OBE). Critics objected to value-laden outcomes that they claimed were inappropriate goals for public schools. "Understanding and appreciating others" was viewed by some as an attempt by the state to endorse "nontraditional" families or homosexual behavior. Some extreme critics believed that schools could be values-free and wanted all values-laden outcomes excised from the curriculum regulations.

The OBE debate in the state, however, failed to disrupt the district's plan to implement character education programs. During the OBE debate, the PTAs in Mt. Lebanon asked the superintendent to explain OBE's relationship to the district's strategic plan. In a series of presentations, the superintendent emphasized that the strategic plan was not related to the new curriculum regulations and had in fact been written a full year before the furor over OBE. He pointed out that the character education initiative in our strategic plan reflected a local decision and was not the result of anything being imposed externally by the state department of education. During this time, fewer than a dozen residents objected to the district's character education initiative in general or any part of it in particular.

The Role of Representative Teams

Since the district's strategic plan describes the process for implementing our character education strategy, it is important to understand the relationship among several parts of the plan. First, the plan contains nine strategies for realizing the district's mission

---

FIGURE 1.1.

Key Teams in the Development Process

Strategic Planning Team

↓

responsible for

↓

Developing a Strategic Plan

including:

A Mission Statement

Nine Strategies for Achieving the Mission

Nine Strategy Teams

↓

responsible for

↓

Writing Action Plans for achieving the strategy

Implementation Teams

↓

responsible for

↓

Implementing Action Plans

statement. After the nine strategies were written, each was assigned to a Strategy Team responsible for writing action plans to achieve the strategy. These nine Strategy Teams each consisted of 20 or more parents, students, school district staff, and members of the school board—thereby increasing community participation from the 28 people who served on the original Strategic Planning Team to more than 200 residents, staff, and students.

After the nine Strategy Teams wrote their action plans, they presented them to the Strategic Planning Team for approval. Most were approved, some with modifications. The nine Strategy Teams produced more than 75 approved action plans. These action plans have been scheduled for implementation over the five-year period of the strategic plan. As each action plan is scheduled for implementation, it is assigned to an administrator who forms an Action Plan Implementation Team. Frequently, this team consists of parents and students in addition to staff.

Lessons Learned

The start-up activities of the Mt. Lebanon School District offer several important lessons.

Lesson 1. Be Prepared to Answer Three Critical Questions: *Why*, *What*, and *How*?

The experience of the school district points up the need to focus on three critical questions as it studies character education and then writes its own program.

1. Why should a school district undertake character education?
2. What are the district's goals in educating for character?
3. How should the district educate for character?

The process for answering these questions should include parents and, where appropriate, students. Ideally, the parents involved in the process should represent the larger community, particularly those who have genuine concerns about schools undertaking this mission.

Why should the school district undertake character education? The district must be absolutely clear about this. You can expect opposition to change, whatever its nature, and emotional opposition to character education from some parents (and staff) who believe that the home should be the sole locus of this undertaking. Be prepared to offer a clear rationale for the school district's role in educating for character. In Mt. Lebanon, growing community support for the effort resulted largely from a compelling rationale for character education that we consistently delivered to parents. The rationale offered three arguments: historical, intrinsic, and social.

Historically, America's schools have viewed character education as one of their basic missions. "Realizing that smart and good are not the same, wise societies since the time of Plato have made moral education a deliberate aim of schooling" (Lickona 1991). Nowhere was that mission more apparent than in the values-laden McGuffey Reader series that was used extensively throughout the land into the early 20th century.

The second argument is that the discussion of values is an intrinsic aspect of teaching. Rules reflect values; the way teachers and administrators treat students reflects values. Discussing the United States Constitution or the Declaration of Independence is a journey into values. Tolerance of cheating represents a value. Expecting students to turn work in on time conveys a value. Discussing Pip's treatment of Joe Gargery in *Great Expectations* exposes Pip's pretentious values.

Teachers and administrators must help parents understand that values-free classrooms and schools do not exist. Thus, the question is not "Should schools teach values?" but "How should schools teach values?" Would parents prefer that teachers carry out their responsibilities as character educators without any planning or direction? Or would they prefer an approach that was developed by the professional staff with community input and was reflective of a set of values with broad community support?

The final element of the rationale for character education is based on the results of surveys that present a disturbing social picture. The Josephson Institute, following a two-year survey of 8,965 adolescents and adults, concluded: "This study shows beyond question that an unacceptably high number of young people act dishonestly or irresponsibly" (Josephson 1992, p. A-3). In 1989 a survey sponsored by the Girl Scouts of America, the Lilly Endowment, and the Mott Foundation asked 90 questions of 5,000 students in grades 4–12: "Their answers reveal a nation of children who do, in fact, have fairly complicated belief systems. But far more often than not, those beliefs run counter to tradition-al values" (Meade 1990, p 40).

What are the district's goals in educating for character? Once it has agreed that character education is an important undertaking, the district must identify its goals. In Mt. Lebanon, our goals were reflected in the strategies—the development of programs for developing ethical and responsible behavior, the creation of car-ing environments in all schools, and the implementation of com-munity service. Our goals were further elaborated by the Strategy Teams that developed action plans for achieving each strategy. The Character Education Strategy Team decided that the heart of its action plans should be a set of core values the district wants to nurture in its students. Chapter 2 examines possible values and processes for identifying them.

How should the district educate for character? Having determined the values the community can support, the next task is to develop ways of nurturing those values through the school's culture and its instructional programs. For each of the three strategies within the original nine strategies (Strategy 2, nurturing ethical and responsible student behavior; Strategy 3, creating caring environ-ments; and Strategy 4, community service), a committee of teach-ers, administrators, parents, and students wrote action plans designed to achieve or implement the strategy.

The scope of the action plans written for Strategy 2, develop-ing programs to nurture the development of ethical and responsi-ble student behavior (referred to from now on as the character education strategy), reflected Tom Lickona's arguments on behalf of comprehensive programs (Lickona 1991). The team responsible for developing action plans for implementing the character edu-cation strategy believed that limiting its efforts to curriculum would be ineffective. *All* elements of the school system must feel responsible for nurturing students' moral development. One characteristic of a comprehensive program would be a school

7

ethos that reflected caring, a critical component of moral behavior. So eventually two Strategy Teams worked on this dimension of character education—the Character Education Strategy Team and the Caring Environment Action Team.

Action plans provided for informing all employees and the community of the strategy, creating a set of core values, implementing those values into the curriculum, developing a district code of ethics for all employees and the school board, writing building-based prosocial behavior codes, and cosponsoring with mental health agencies character education parenting programs. (Subsequent chapters provide information about each aspect of a comprehensive program.)

Another characteristic of a comprehensive program is a conceptualization of what a moral being is. Mt. Lebanon focused its attention on educating the head, heart, and hand. Children need to know what is right, to feel obligated to do what is right, and to act on that combination of knowledge and feeling (Lickona 1991).

Lesson 2. Develop a Communications Plan for Informing the Community and All Employees.

Because we made a conscious effort to inform the community at all stages of the process, support for our plan grew. The communication process was so critical that an entire Action Plan was devoted to it. Details of that plan are described in Chapter 3.

Lesson 3. Character Education Requires Strong Leadership at the Central Office and Building Levels.

Significant change such as implementing character education usually creates concern and is likely to generate some opposition. *In Search of Excellence* presents the case for having an "executive champion" to help navigate the ship of change through stormy waters:

> The successful executive champion's . . . been there—been through the lengthy process of husbanding, seen what it takes to shield a potential practical new idea from the organization's formal tendency toward negation (Peters and Waterman 1982, p. 208).

In a school district, the executive champion should be someone who has:

- Influence with the board of school directors and community
- Access to district funds
- The interpersonal skills necessary to building a critical mass of support
- The authority to make things happen

Ideally, the superintendent would play the role, but realistically, superintendents often don't have the time required for this task. An assistant superintendent, director of instruction, or principal is a more likely candidate, especially if that individual was a key player in the district's early discussions of the initiative.

If the superintendent can't lead the effort, the community must see him or her as a committed supporter of character education and as the person who serves as the district's executive champion of the effort. As Assistant Superintendent, I became our district's champion of character education. As part of that role, I chaired the Character Education Strategy Team that wrote the action plans for the strategy, and I have since chaired three of the Character Education Action Plan Implementation Teams. I have also made presentations to most of our PTAs and a number of civic groups.

After the implementation of Heartwood, our elementary character education program, I observed a number of classes and taught several so I would be able to speak from a firsthand point of view. I also conducted follow-up discussions with the faculties of the first two schools to implement Heartwood to obtain feedback about its implementation, an activity that one teacher said was important as a signal of central office commitment to the program. I have also participated in the staff development of the other five elementary faculties as they implemented the program.

Individual principals must also play a leadership role. Their staff and community must view them as committed to character education. This commitment involves participating in planning activities, presenting the programs to parent groups, talking with students about the undertaking, providing staff development, modeling the values of the program, customizing the program for each school, and ensuring follow-up support and accountability through supervision.

Lesson 4. Seek Community and Staff Consensus

Initiatives for change can come from a variety of sources: federal or state mandates, school board directives, pressure groups, planning processes, formal or informal program evaluations, suggestions from individuals or departments or faculties, or in the case of the Mt. Lebanon School District, a study group.

Whatever the source, if the initiative is going to succeed, it must achieve a critical mass of support or consensus among the stakeholders. Certainly this includes the school board, professional staff, and parents and parent groups such as the PTA. In Mt. Lebanon, the grass-roots study group of 10 teachers, administrators, and parents found ways to reach increasingly larger audiences. Their initial effort produced the Lickona visit, which reached an audience of 100 teachers in the voluntary inservice program and 700 parents through the PTA seminar. The strategic planning effort followed and through the Strategic Planning Team, the Strategy Teams, and Action Plan Implementation Teams, more than 200 residents, staff members, and students became involved in the character education effort. The Communications Action Plan, described in Chapter 3, reached all of the district's staff and the community's 40,000 residents several times.

Lesson 5. Seek Visible and Substantive Support from the School Board.

The board must show its support early and in some concrete, visible form. Without it, the program will have little chance of thriving. Such support could assume one of several forms:

• A character education component in a board-approved district strategic or long-range plan

• A character education goal among the district's instructional goals

• A district policy on character education

• A resolution supporting a character education initiative

• Board participation in character education activities. A member of the Mt. Lebanon school board served on the Character Education Strategy Team. In Burlington, North Carolina, at the beginning of a character education service workshop, the school board president welcomed the staff and endorsed the character education initiative.

As new members join the school board, the board orientation program must provide information about the history and substance of the school's character education initiative. In Mt. Lebanon, within three years of the development of the District's Strategic Plan that included the character education strategy, six of the school board members who had approved the Plan had left the board. Initially, we failed to provide the new members with information about our character education initiative, assuming that the community information program had provided the knowledge they needed as school board members. The questions and concerns of several new members of the board revealed the error of our assumption.

Reflecting on our "getting started" process, I have to admit we were fortunate. We did not have a vision of a successful implementation process at first. What served us well in the absence of that vision was a district tradition of involving different audiences in decision making. It was through that tradition that we brought increasingly larger numbers of people into the process until we finally reached a critical mass of support that enabled us to move from the question of *Why undertake character education?* to the issues of goals and means described in the following chapters.

2

Core Values

The Mt. Lebanon School District Character Education Strategy Team quickly decided that the heart of the strategy should be a set of core values. The values would be integrated into each action plan. Therefore, in writing the curriculum action plan, team members directed that those responsible for implementing the plan must weave the values into the curriculum. The district's employee code of ethics had to reflect the core values. Each school's prosocial behavior code had to reflect the core values. The character education parenting programs had to be built on the core values.

Having decided what role the values would play in the action plans, the team next turned its attention to the process for developing the core. They began by brainstorming those values that reflected broad community support. After listing more than 40 values that the community would support, they began the arduous task of defining and combining. Fearing that a long list would overwhelm those responsible for integrating them into the action plans, their goal was to generate a handful that students and staff could reasonably be expected to recite quickly if asked to list the district's values.

The next step involved deciding which values the schools could nurture with community support and which to exclude based on obvious and serious potential for controversy. For example, team members saw that the value "respect for the environment" would be one that environmentalists and industrialists would dispute in terms of its concrete application. Consequently, they decided to exclude such a specific value in favor of the broader values listed here.

When these discussions of definitions and attempts to reduce the length of the list began to produce a great deal of frustration, I asked the team members if they wanted to examine value statements from other sources. In the spring of 1991, the group reviewed several sets of values and finally agreed to adopt the value statements prepared by the 1988 ASCD Panel on Moral Education. They concluded that the ASCD values and substatements, with minor modifications, reflected the essence of their original list.

Core Values of the Mt. Lebanon School District

The following core values are a statement of belief of the Mt. Lebanon School District. The substatements following each core value are a resource to guide the school community as they make decisions about how the core values will be integrated in the school district's programs.

We believe that the morally mature person habitually:

1. **Respects human dignity, which includes**
   - internalizing the responsibility to protect and extend the worth and rights of all persons,
   - avoiding deception and dishonesty,
   - promoting human equality,
   - respecting freedom of conscience,
   - working with people of different views,
   - refraining from prejudiced actions, and
   - respecting public and private property.

2. **Demonstrates active responsibility for the welfare of others, which includes,**
   - engaging in altruistic acts for impersonal others and the common good,
   - recognizing interdependence among people,
   - caring for one's country,
   - seeking social justice,
   - taking pleasure in helping others, and
   - working to help others reach moral maturity.

3. **Integrates individual interests and social responsibilities, which includes**
   - displaying self-regarding and other-regarding moral virtues: self-control, diligence, fairness, honesty, civility in everyday life,

13

- becoming involved in community life,
- embracing the responsibilities of a citizen in a democratic society, fulfilling commitments,
- developing self-esteem through relationships with others, and
- recognizing a measure of self-worth is what one does for the betterment of society and future generations.

4. Demonstrates integrity, which includes,
- taking stands for moral principles,
- practicing honesty and truthfulness,
- displaying moral courage,
- accepting responsibility for one's choices,
- seeing one's work as an extension of oneself, and
- recognizing self-esteem and self-worth results from real achievement in surmounting challenges and obstacles in learning and life experiences.

5. Applies moral principles when making choices and judgments, which includes
- recognizing the moral issues involved in a situation,
- thinking about the moral consequences of decisions,
- seeking to be informed about important moral issues in society and the world, and
- holding these core values as a standard measuring one's own behavior, the behavior of others, the behavior of authority, the behavior of public authority.

6. Seeks peaceful resolution of conflict, which includes
- striving for the fair resolution of personal and social conflicts,
- knowing when to compromise and when to confront,
- avoiding physical and verbal aggression, and
- working for peace.

In general, the morally mature person understands moral principles and accepts responsibility for applying them.

This statement of core values encountered opposition on two occasions. First, two members of the Strategic Planning Team objected to the substatements, arguing that some were too vague and, therefore, potentially controversial. For example, the substatement "caring for one's country" could take the form of civil disobedience or blind obedience to bad policy. The other objection came from the Action Plan Implementation Team responsible for integrating the values into the curriculum. They noted that the document was too long and recommended a list of single-word core values. The Character Education Planning Team, which had developed the core values and action plans, reconvened to consider the objections.

They began by considering the core attributes of the Heartwood Institute (Courage, Loyalty, Justice, Respect, Hope, Honesty, and Love) and the Six Pillars of Character of the Josephson Institute of Ethics (Trustworthiness, Respect, Responsibility, Caring, Fairness, and Citizenship).

After considerable discussion, the Character Education Planning Team decided to keep their original core value statements. Recognizing the potential for controversy that the substatements created, they agreed to use only the six main statements for public presentations. They directed that the substatements be given to all of the committees integrating the core values into their action plans as a means of providing those committees with a sense of how the Character Education Strategy Team saw the core values being translated into more specific behavior.

They revised the introduction to the values and emphasized that the substatements were offered as information about the Planning Team's view of the values and as a "resource to guide" using the values in the implementation of action plans. They decided that any subgroup or committee working with the core values would have to go through the process of defining the core values in ways that made them applicable to specific grade levels and subjects.

Lessons Learned

The experience of the Mt. Lebanon School District offers the following lessons in developing a set of core values:

Lesson 1. Clarify What Is Meant by Values.

Keep in mind that the values should drive the rest of the program. Therefore, take care in selecting and defining them. Early in the development of our core, it would have been useful to have people define what they meant by values and to offer examples of their own values. Most people will define values in a character education context to mean highly regarded behaviors or attitudes. Typically, their examples will include such things as honesty, respect, good manners, courage, education. These values will probably fall into two categories: moral values and nonmoral values/social conventions. Lickona defines moral values as ones that carry an obligation, as opposed to nonmoral values, which carry no obligation:

> We feel obligated to keep a promise, pay our bills, care for our children, and be fair in our dealings with others. Moral values tell us what we *ought* to do. We must abide by them even when we'd rather not (Lickona 1991).

Somewhat similar to Lickona's view of moral and nonmoral values is the distinction between morality and social convention (Nucci 1989). Social conventions such as styles of dress and forms of addressing each other are the arbitrary and changeable standards of social behavior agreed upon by the members of a group (Turiel 1983). In one sense, they do carry an obligation; that is, to abide by the conventions or manners of that society. However, morality carries a different kind of obligation. "In contrast with conventions, moral considerations are not arbitrary but stem from factors intrinsic to actions; consequences such as harm to others" (Nucci 1989, p.184).

Schools should probably focus their attention on identifying values that fall into the moral domain. That suggestion, however, does not preclude attention to social convention or manners (such as greeting people courteously), especially when such manners can be seen as having a moral dimension related to core values such as respect and caring. Chapter 5 elaborates the role of social conventions or manners in a comprehensive character education program.

Lesson 2. Develop the Core Values with a Process That Produces Ownership.

Chapter 1 lists three questions school districts need to answer as they plan and implement character education programs:

1. Why should a school district undertake character education? (rationale)

2. What are the district's goals in educating for character? (core values)

3. How should the district educate for character? (specific programs)

Although community participation is important to all three steps, it is absolutely critical in identifying the core values. Participation should reflect the diversity of the community. In developing its core values, Baltimore County's Values Education Task Force met with a fundamentalist minister and a representative of the ACLU to obtain diverse perspectives (Saterlie 1992). That step anticipated what often occurs in the creation of character education programs: someone will object that a values education program will cause the state (in this case, schools) to violate the Constitution's First Amendment anti-establishment clause. While many of the values developed by school districts will in fact have values that are also embraced by religious groups, those with no religious affiliation will usually embrace the core if the values presented cut across belief systems, as we can see from what happened in Baltimore County:

> The minister asked, "If you are going to teach values in 'state schools,' who or what will be your moral example?" He held the Bible in his right hand and described his concept of Jesus Christ. Clearly the issue of the separation of church and state had to be addressed. But we were reminded by the ACLU's representative that the works of Confucius, Plato, Aristotle and other philosophers make it clear that morality resides in all aspects of human behavior and cannot be tied to any specific religion (Saterlie 1992, p. 1).

The Baltimore County Values Education Task Force resolved the issue by using the Constitution as the source of the values. It selected 24 values that, in its judgment, are either explicit or implicit in the Constitution:

- Compassion
- Courtesy
- Critical Inquiry
- Due Process
- Equality of Opportunity
- Freedom of Thought and Action
- Honesty
- Human Worth and Dignity
- Integrity
- Justice
- Knowledge
- Loyalty
- Objectivity
- Order
- Patriotism
- Rational Consent
- Reasoned Argument
- Respect for Others' Rights
- Responsibility
- Responsible Citizenship
- Rule of Law
- Self-Respect
- Tolerance
- Truth

Concern over church-state relations sometimes causes school officials to overlook the input of clerical associations in developing core values. Clergy can be useful and appropriate resources, as Baltimore County acknowledged. The Fox Chapel School District of Pennsylvania and the Burlington City School District of North Carolina have asked their clerical associations to assist in the development of a list of values that would be acceptable to members of all faiths.

Many writers, organizations, and school districts have developed sets of core values. They range from Lickona's focus on respect and responsibility (Lickona 1991) to Baltimore County's Constitutionally-derived list of 24. A district that adopts or adapts a set of values developed externally should do so only after brainstorming its own list. A planning committee needs to understand firsthand the dynamics of developing a set of core values if it is to explain the process to its constituents. To adopt someone else's core values without first identifying which values are important locally is both foolhardy and insensitive.

Lesson 3. It's Easier to Name Values in the Abstract Than to Define Them in the Concrete.

Selecting values that appear to have broad community support can create a sense of false security. While most people can accept values such as honesty and courage, the terms are highly abstract. Once people begin to use them in designing programs, the terms must be made less abstract. Expect lively discussion as that occurs. *Courage* as defined by elementary teachers in a developmentally appropriate way may not be quite the same as the definition cast by a high school social studies department. Several ideas are important to remember as subgroups begin to work with the values:

1. The value has to be defined in a way that meets the needs of the subgroup. If that doesn't occur, student needs will not be met and the subgroup will feel no ownership of the value.

2. Defining a value in terms of observable human behavior is sometimes difficult. Probably the best illustration of that process appears in the 20th issue of the journal *Ethics: Easier Said Than Done*, published by the Josephson Institute of Ethics. This issue

contains portions of the discussions that occurred within the group that produced the Six Pillars of Character (Hanson 1992).

3. To avoid acrimony in defining terms, each member of the group needs to manifest the values he or she is attempting to define. If a group that is attempting to define *caring* fails to manifest that quality in determining the application of the term to a program, then some intervention is needed.

Lesson 4. Avoiding Controversy in Selecting and Defining Values May Ultimately Be a Disservice to Students and Society.

Earlier, I discussed the desire of the Strategic Planning Team to avoid values that might be viewed as controversial. But a values curriculum that seeks to avoid controversy may be so bland that it has no positive influence on students. As I have reflected on that decision, several important points emerged.

First, controversial topics are already being discussed in most school districts. In some instances, the written curriculum calls for this to occur. In other situations, the discussions are part of the *taught* curriculum; that is, although a topic is not included in the written curriculum, teachers have decided that it warrants consideration. Also, students through their questions will often dictate that certain topics be considered. The absence of any furor over this in most communities is probably a testament to the ability of teachers to handle these topics responsibly and to the community's recognition that it is desirable for students at some appropriate age to begin wrestling with the difficult questions that will engage them as voting citizens.

Second, almost any value will have the potential to elicit some negative reaction or concern. One example of this is Mt. Lebanon's value of seeking peaceful resolution of conflict, which has prompted some staff and parents to ask if discussions of concrete applications of the value will put students at risk in certain situations. Will a child who acquires the value of peaceful resolution of conflict in one environment manifest a naivete in a different environment by pursuing a solution that will provoke someone who doesn't share the value to respond violently? In that context, some staff and parents are concerned about the direction students will receive in applying the core value.

Third, we must consider the implications of a district's decision to avoid controversy. Tom Lickona asks schools to think about:

> The educational implication of a district policy that seeks to avoid all potentially controversial values in formulating its policy and goals. What about the need to prepare students, especially at the high school level, to reason about conflicting values . . . , which they will have to do as members of a democratic society whose ongoing moral development occurs at least partly because of ethical and public policy debates such as the abortion controversy (Lickona 1993).

I do not advocate as a long-term goal or policy the avoidance of values that some may see as controversial. To do so would run counter to the plea I am making for transformational leadership. On the other hand, I recognize that a school district may initially need to avoid some value, or the specific application of some value, until there is greater community support for and understanding of a school's character education program. The absence of such support or understanding could prove fatal to the larger character education effort. When communities have arrived at a point where there is support for the teaching of controversial topics, Lickona recommends the writing of school board-approved guidelines for the instruction (Lickona 1991).

Lesson 5. Consider Creating a Short List of Single-Word Core Values.

In Mt. Lebanon, the Curriculum Action Plan Implementation Team asked the Character Education Strategy Team, which developed the core values, to consider revising them into a set of values that could be represented by single words. The Curriculum Team believed that single-word values would have greater utility because they could be recalled more easily. Teachers who had piloted the Heartwood Program liked its list of seven core attributes because each attribute was identified with a single word. The Character Education Strategy Team rejected the Curriculum Team's request because they liked the way in which the substatements of their list elaborated the value. The Strategy Team should have compromised by reducing each of the six main statements to a single word and including the substatements as a means of conveying their sense of the value's essential spirit. Reducing "Respects human dignity" to "Respect" would not have damaged the intent of that value as long as substatements illustrating the value were included.

A short list is also less daunting to staff as they implement the values into all facets of a school system. A set of values as long as Baltimore's poses a challenge to a district that wants its students and staff to commit the values to memory. Further, at the beginning of planning a program, a long list may strike a staff as imposing too much change. A short list of single-word values with substatements elaborating the values can accomplish as much, if not more, than a long list of values.

Lesson 6. Core Values Should Substantially Affect the School District's Operations.

Those responsible for planning and implementing a character education program should ask themselves what it is they expect their effort to achieve. If their goal is to influence a school's or a school systems's ethos through a comprehensive character education effort, they should identify the changes they hope to see as a result of their efforts. The core values should be a major consideration in this collective reflection, for they can either exert substantial influence or cause embarrassment. The embarrassment will occur if the district merely gives lip service to the values rather than uses them to influence decision making and other forms of behavior. Incongruence between a district's core values and its operation represents one of the biggest obstacles to the successful implementation of a character education program.

Given that possibility, the staff should seek challenging situations that represent meaningful tests of the district's commitment to the values. Labor-management relations provide such a challenging opportunity to examine a school district's commitment to realizing a difference through character education. For example, a school district near Mt. Lebanon experienced a bitter teachers strike that deeply divided the community, a situation the residents and staff of Mt. Lebanon hope they can avoid when they negotiate their next contract with teachers. Before negotiations begin, both sides should discuss what implications their core values have for the negotiations, especially how they will treat each

21

other at the bargaining table and in their public pronouncements. If they can agree on negotiating parameters that reflect the core values, they should then appoint an independent observer who can provide both sides with feedback about their success in following the values-based negotiating parameters.

Core values can be viewed as something written primarily for students or they can be seen as something that speaks to all members of the school community. They can become a sheet of paper that people ignore or a presence that prompts people to pause in their decision making. They can become an embarrassment or a source of pride. In short, the degree of their influence will be the ultimate barometer of a character education program's success.

3

Communications

Our Character Education Strategy Team felt that the need to inform the community and staff was sufficiently important to warrant writing an action plan for just that purpose. They had four reasons for viewing communications as a critical element.

The Importance of Communicating with Community and Staff

Much of the debate over new curriculum reforms in the state had resulted from the values in the state-mandated student outcomes statements. Some critics charged that the commonwealth was trying to insinuate "politically correct" ideas into the reform program through values-laden outcome statements. The Character Education Strategy Planning Team believed that presentations to our community and staff would create an atmosphere of openness and trust that had been absent in discussions in other school districts of the state's reform agenda.

In addition, the Mt. Lebanon School District had a tradition of active parent involvement in the schools. Our parents and other community members expected our schools to communicate proactively. Critics of schools sometimes charge, with justification, that programs are introduced without informing parents. Parents in Mt. Lebanon needed to know the details of our character education strategy.

Second, all students and employees would eventually be affected by the strategy. With the goal of emphasizing an ethos of caring and responsibility throughout the system, we were going to ask the entire staff to model the core values. Further, we would also ask for their help in developing a district code of ethics as a visible commitment to the core.

Third, the prominence of character education in the district's strategic plan suggested community and staff support had reached a critical mass. Presentation of the specific action plans would provide an opportunity to test that assumption. The communications program confirmed that conclusion: typically, parents who attended the character education presentations expressed approval and asked how soon they could expect to see programs in their own schools.

Finally, the character education strategy included action plans that needed staff or parent volunteers to serve on implementation teams. The information program became a means of recruiting people for those teams.

The Communications Action Plan

Our Communications Action Plan had three major elements. First, it called for a presentation to all employees. On an inservice day, all employees, with the exception of the head and night custodians, participated in a presentation of the district's character education strategy. The head custodians remained in their buildings to handle emergencies. The morning program was videotaped for them and the night custodians to view later. All telephone calls were forwarded to three central office numbers where substitute secretaries were assigned. Cafeteria workers, who normally would have been home on an inservice day, were paid for the two hours the program required. These extraordinary arrangements for the morning's inservice program conveyed the high priority district leaders had given to character education.

Once again, the district turned to Tom Lickona as a speaker who could present an inspirational rationale for character education. Before the keynote speech, the superintendent endorsed the character education strategy. I then presented the core values and the details of the action plans. After the keynote speech, while teachers and administrators heard a presentation on another topic, Lickona met with the classified employees of the district (all employees other than teachers and administrators) to discuss their role in the character education strategy.

The second element of the communications plan called for a community presentation. In order to attract as large a crowd as possible, the school district entered into a partnership with a local mental health agency to make its overview of character education part of a parenting program on the same topic. Because of the large turnout for Lickona's PTA program two years earlier, he was asked to present the program. As with the staff communications program, I presented the core values and action plans before the keynote speech.

The third element called for the creation of a handout that could be expanded into a resource book later as action plans were implemented. The handout provided:

- A history of the district's study of character education
- The broader elements of the district's strategic plan (beliefs, the mission statement, objectives, parameters, and nine strategies)
- Action plans for the character education strategy
- Definitions of key terms (moral, ethics, character, values, and social conventions)
- A summary of major schools of thought on educating for character
- The statement of ethics of the American Association for School Administrators
- A list of resources and specific programs
- A bibliography

Assuming that not every employee would read all of the 40-page handout, the planners decided to duplicate 150 for those who wanted them. They were made available after the program, and when the supply was exhausted, approximately 100 employees requested copies. Almost 50 percent of the employee group had elected to look at some portion of the handout. Once again, interest in character education continued at a high level.

Lessons Learned

Lesson 1. Make Certain the Scope of the Communications Program Is Adequate.

As it turned out, the scope of the written Communications Action Plan was inadequate. Fortunately, we recognized early that we needed to include more activities. For example, the original plan called for one presentation to the entire employee group and one presentation to the community. After those initial presentations, we realized we needed to provide an ongoing flow of information about character education. Therefore, we created additional means for informing our community and staff.

Our Communications Plan emphasized the importance of an "executive champion." In that role, I offered to deliver the keynote speech at the PTA Council's annual spring workshop. This character education speech to approximately 200 people produced invitations to make similar presentations to the individual PTA building units.

The district's strategic plan provided other opportunities to present the details of the character education strategy. Annually, the superintendent presented a community update on the strategic plan; those updates included information on the three character education-related strategies (character education, caring environment, and community service). Further, the district's newsletter and annual performance report provided information on character education and were effective communications tools since they reached every home in the district.

As we entered the second year of the strategic plan, I wondered whether employee interest in the character education strategy remained high. I prepared a memo summarizing some of the national developments that were occurring in character education and sent one to every employee. Those who wanted to continue receiving information about character education at the local, regional, and national levels were invited to become part of a character education mailing list. More than 170 employees signed up. That network has evolved into a district character education newsletter I publish quarterly. Circulation has grown to almost 200 employees and I have been able to reduce my writing responsibilities as employees submit articles.

Interestingly enough, the original plan included activities to inform the staff and community, yet no plans were developed for the people most directly affected by the undertaking—the students. No discussion of whether it would be appropriate to inform students of the character education strategy ever took place.

Now it seems obvious, given the amount of strategic planning activity that occurred within the community and the importance of the undertaking, that a lesson on the district's strategic planning activities could have been integrated into both the elementary and secondary social studies programs in developmentally appropriate ways. We missed a wonderful opportunity to describe to our students how participatory government works at the local level and to talk about how local values get translated into specific programs. Chapter 4 provides suggestions for informing students of the initiative.

Also, the Communications Action Plan did not include providing information to the community once specific elements of the character education strategy were implemented. For example, the Curriculum Action Plan Implementation Team was responsible for studying ways of integrating the core values into the curriculum. However, once it began its work and decided to use the Heartwood Program at the elementary level, there was no plan for introducing the curriculum to the community. Recognizing that, the Implementation Team worked with the principals and PTAs of each school to plan community presentations. These presentations are critical for building parent support for the program and for helping parents and others in the community to understand the nature of the readings, methodologies, and evaluation procedures. We found that after we conducted these presentations, parent acceptance of the program was extremely high.

The benefit of our communications effort became apparent when the state department of education decided to make outcome-based education part of their reform agenda and values education became a political issue. At that point, our community knew that values education in Mt. Lebanon had been a local decision made as part of strategic planning and was not the result of a state mandate. A significant number of residents had been involved in that planning process. Further, they had heard a compelling rationale for the school district's role as a partner with parents in educating for character.

Lesson 2. Follow Up the Initial Communications with Classified Employees.

The Communications Action Plan wrongly assumed that a morning's presentation of the district's character education strategy to the classified employees would produce commitment to modeling the core values. Immediately after the opening 90-minute session for all employees, Tom Lickona met with just the classified employees to discuss their role in the character education strategy. The lively discussion produced a list of concerns and opportunities that cried for some form of follow-up. For instance, cafeteria workers complained about the insensitivity that students conveyed when they made disparaging remarks about food in the presence of workers who took pride in their food preparation. One cafeteria worker suggested that they wear name tags so that students might begin to understand that they were more than "nameless food servers."

The district, however, had no action plan for building upon the initial enthusiasm of the classified employees, many of whom had been so vocal in sharing ideas with Lickona. A year later, when the call went out to union leaders to recruit a member to serve on the district committee that would write a district code of ethics, the president of the foodworkers' union could not find a member willing to serve on the Ethics Action Plan Implementation Team.

Lesson 3. Communicate the Priority of Character Education.

The history of change in education is not impressive. Many innovations have been allowed to wither on the vine because they have not been nurtured. Educators seem to move from one innovation to another so quickly that few receive the support required to make them part of the institution. Character education as an initiative certainly faces this problem.

As our character education strategy was introduced to the staff, many understandably assumed that this, too, would pass. The unusual arrangement of bringing the entire employee group together for a presentation of the district's core values and character education action plans was designed to communicate the importance of the district's character education strategy. But that approach must be supplemented with other means of communicating character education's high priority. Chapter 6 provides examples of how this message can be conveyed through a school district's employee recruitment, employee evaluation, and staff development programs.

Lesson 4. Do Not Dismiss Critics Quickly.

When the school reform/outcome-based education firestorm occurred in Pennsylvania, much of the opposition came from critics viewed as Christian Fundamentalists or extreme political conservatives. Educators and reform critics characterized each other in antagonistic terms and used heavy-handed strategies to make their case with the public.

Educators must never lose sight of the need to *honestly* assess the validity of the arguments offered by critics of values education. Some educators succumbed to the temptation to dismiss out-of-hand the critics of school reform and OBE as off-the-wall extremists. While I was concerned about the tactics used by some critics of school reform and OBE, I had to acknowledge that some of their concerns struck a responsive chord in my parental heart. They expressed concern over schools' educating for "politically correct" attitudes in such controversial areas as human sexuality and abortion. Further, they feared that state-mandated assessment systems would penalize students for holding certain values.

Seemingly innocent and well-intentioned means of pursuing instructional objectives can often create parental concern. In one school district, the 9th grade English teachers created a list of questions designed to give students "food for thought" as they generated topics for compositions. One parent called and objected to the question "Do you receive enough spending money from your family?" She pointed out that the schools had no business inviting students to write about such personal matters. She added that she and her husband believed that it was wrong to indulge their children's desire for material things to the same extent as other parents, and her children would probably feel that they never received enough money from mom and dad.

Many of the concerns expressed by critics of educational reform address important policy issues at the national, state, and local levels. Any school district undertaking character education programs should understand parents' concerns and be able to respond in terms of district policy and practice. Most important in responding to critics, schools should model the respect for persons that is central to any good character education program.

No communications plan for a character education program can be considered a discrete task with a beginning and an end. The need to communicate will be continuous, although communications can probably drop to a lower level once the program has been fully implemented and has become an accepted part of the district's continuing programs.

4

Curriculum Strategy

If core values represent the heart of a character education program, then the curriculum is its head. Clearly, one of the goals of a character education curriculum must be to have students think about the core values and how they get translated into behavior.

Mt. Lebanon's Curriculum Action Plan Implementation Team was responsible for finding ways to integrate the core values into the existing curriculum. To start, team members considered several elements prescribed by the district's Character Education Strategy Team:

1. The core values must be integrated into the existing curriculum.

2. The general instructional approach must reflect a synthesis of the stage development and behaviorist schools of thought.

3. A variety of programs already in operation throughout the country must be examined in developing a specific curriculum.

Integrating Core Values into the Existing Curriculum

The Curriculum Action Plan called for integration rather than the creation of a separate curriculum. At the elementary level, the daily schedule did not permit adding new content. At the secondary level, the schedule presented a similar problem: creating an additional required course for students would further reduce the time available for electives. Further, an ethics elective would reach only a small portion of the student body and thereby fail to convey the priority of values in the curriculum. Therefore, our curriculum plan called for all courses to reinforce the core values in ways that (1) met the developmental needs of students and (2) took advantage of the values opportunities inherent in each subject area.

Reflecting Stages of Development and Behaviorism in Instruction

The district's character education strategy directed the Curriculum Implementation Action Team to develop an approach that synthesized the stages of development and behaviorist schools of thought. In writing the action plans, members of the Character Education Strategy Team had investigated the various schools of thought on educating for character. On the one hand, they found educators like Lawrence Kohlberg (1984) who describe moral development in terms of six stages; moral education consists, in part, of helping students move through these stages. Another school of thought, represented by educators such as William Bennett (Damon 1988), concentrates on giving students examples of exemplary behavior through the study of literature and history, expecting school employees to model positive values, reinforcing appropriate behavior, and disciplining inappropriate actions.

The Character Education Strategy Team concluded that nurturing the moral development of the young required attention to both reason and behavior modification. Accordingly, it specified that the curriculum address both. Like Spinoza, team members came to believe that "the palace of reason may be entered only through the courtyard of habit." Lickona's *Educating for Character* provided numerous ideas for an approach that integrated the stage development and behaviorist schools of thought.

Examining Character Education Programs Already in Operation

The Character Education Strategy Team directed the Curriculum Implementation Action Team to review a number of character education programs already in operation throughout the country. These included the Child Development Project and the programs offered by Baltimore County, the Thomas Jefferson Institute, and the Heartwood Institute.

The Team had an opportunity to examine the Heartwood Program within the school district. Independent of the character education strategy, one of the elementary principals in Mt. Lebanon had learned of Heartwood and had obtained central office permission to pilot the program. Heartwood, a multicultural, literature-based curriculum, uses classic children's stories from around the world to foster seven core attributes: courage, loyalty, justice, respect, hope, honesty, and love.

The Implementation Team conferred with the faculty that piloted Heartwood and concluded that its literature-based approach would work best for the elementary portion of the curriculum plan. The program had several attractive elements. First, as a literature-based program it could be integrated into the existing reading program without any serious disruption of the schedule.

Second, the approach used stories, a universal medium for teaching values. Humans acquire important moral lessons in a variety of ways. Probably the most effective is firsthand experience. One of the least effective is merely telling someone that he or she "should" behave in a certain manner. Literature offers a happy middle ground: It speaks to the head through the heart as the reader vicariously experiences life's lessons. As Flannery O'Connor has observed, "A Story is a way to say something that can't be said any other way ... " (Kilpatrick 1992).

The third appeal of Heartwood was the ease with which it could be implemented. The teachers found it to be user-friendly. Elementary teachers typically have received considerable preparation in teaching reading. That fact combined with the prominent role of reading in most schools gives teachers a high comfort level with children's literature. In addition, special subject teachers in areas like art and music found they could tie into Heartwood. For example, a music teacher taught two songs a month that correlated with one or more of the following Heartwood elements: the attribute, the story, or the ethnic group from which the story originated. Since one of the creators of Heartwood was a retired elementary teacher, the resource guide's suggestions for introducing the stories and discussing them after the reading reflected practical approaches. At the end of the pilot year, the teachers and principal concluded that the program could be implemented with as little as five hours of initial staff development.

Finally, the home extension activities proved to be an attractive feature. Heartwood wants parents to know what the schools are doing with values. Consequently, the program provides activities that give parents the opportunity to hear from their children what they have read and discussed in class. It allows parents to give the attribute their own shading. Following a story on hope, for example, the class might be asked to discuss the story with their families and to identify two nonmaterial things they are hoping for during the coming year.

The Curriculum Implementation Action Team next turned its attention to the junior high or middle school level. The success of Heartwood at the elementary level prompted them to take a similar approach at the junior high school level. Using a foundation grant, the school's junior high school language arts department and the Heartwood Institute developed a junior high school/middle school version of the program. Like the elementary version, the junior high program includes home extension activities designed to involve parents in discussions of the core attributes.

The Curriculum Implementation Action Team did not want to restrict the secondary-level efforts to the junior high language arts curriculum. Committee members believed that other subject areas at the junior high school and high school offered rich natural opportunities to relate content to the core values. They decided to devote most of one year's inservice time to having all secondary departments review their curriculums and identify areas where they could draw a specific connection to a core value.

Other than the junior high school language arts department, however, the rest of the secondary faculty had had no contact with the core values for the year following the overview of the character education strategy. Therefore, the Curriculum Implementation Action Team decided to initiate the curricular activity of the other departments with another keynote speaker. This time, the district turned to a demographer who presented a gloomy picture of the present through a wide array of statistics. For example, more teenage boys die of gunshots than from all natural causes combined. Or, 40 Pennsylvania students died of abuse in 1988. More than 900 drug-addicted babies are born in the United States every day. He challenged the district to become part of a national effort to change the negative social trends he had identified.

After the keynote speech, the faculty met in interdepartmental small groups to discuss the implications of the findings for their work. In this setting, they identified the values they hoped to see in their high school graduates. They next met as departments to decide how they might address some of the social trends through conscious attention to the core values within their respective curriculums.

Following the inservice program, teachers and administrators evaluated the keynote address and the small-group follow-up activities. The evaluation helped the district assess staff attitudes one year after they were presented with an overview of the district's character education strategy.

Several important points emerged through the assessment of the inservice. First, after one year, the support of the secondary faculty for the strategy continued at an extremely high level. Second, teachers expressed concern about how to integrate values into the curriculum. Third, the staff revealed a need for inservice to train teachers to nurture the development of those values. Similarly, a number of responses emphasized the importance of teachers' modeling the core values, a concern that would be addressed through the action plan prescribing employee codes of ethics.

Finally, the middle school teachers identified character traits they wanted to see in Mt. Lebanon's graduates, and these were found to be consonant with the district's core values.

At first glance, the two sets of values, listed in Figure 4.1, may appear to be different, but when one includes the substatements for the district's six values, they are quite similar. Honesty, for example, while absent from the six general statements of Mt. Lebanon's core values, was listed in the substatements for Core Value 3: Integrates individual interests and social responsibilities. Further, while work ethic was absent as a separate value, it was implicit in the substatements for several of the district core values: for example, diligence, fulfilling responsibilities, seeing one's work as an extension of oneself.

FIGURE 4.1
Desirable Values to Nurture in Students

District-Identified Core Values

1. Respects human dignity
2. Demonstrates active responsibility for the welfare of others
3. Integrates individual interests and social responsibilities
4. Demonstrates integrity
5. Applies moral principles when making choices and judgments
6. Seeks peaceful resolution of conflict

Teacher-Identified Values for Graduates

1. Honesty
2. Caring for others; compassion
3. Work ethic
4. Integrity
5. Responsibility for one's actions
6. Self-esteem
7. Ethics
8. Respect for others
9. Acceptance of others

Lessons Learned

Lesson 1. Create a Context for Integrating Core Values.

The integration of the core values into the existing curriculum raises an important question: What is the larger context for the integration of the values? What larger context will a secondary science teacher reference as she discusses the relationship between a science issue and a district core value?

The need for a larger context struck me as I observed Heartwood lessons. Teacher questions asked students to think about the events of a story, to reflect on how they felt at particular points, and to consider what effect the discussion of a story might have on their behavior. For example, after discussing the Heartwood attribute *respect* during October, a 6th grade teacher asked the class what effect their discussions should have on their behavior during the coming Halloween weekend. In a subsequent discussion, the teacher observed that it would have been helpful to have a developmentally appropriate concept of moral or good behavior to draw upon. Some might argue that such a discussion of respect is sufficient unto itself and needs no larger context. Given the character education goals of the Mt. Lebanon School District, however, the absence of a larger context represents a shortcoming.

The core values are part of a larger picture students need to understand. That larger picture or context offers three elements students should grasp at some point in their schooling:

• *A concept of the moral person as including the head (knowing what is right), the heart (caring about what is right), and the hand (doing what is right).* Students should understand that the district is trying to influence those three dimensions of character and be challenged to act on what they know and feel to be right. In Mt. Lebanon, the challenge to act should be tied to Core Value 5: Applies moral principles when making choices and judgments.

• *The larger social picture that prompted the district to undertake character education.* In presenting the social picture that prompted the district to undertake a character education program, teachers should draw students into an analysis of conditions, such as the increase in violent crimes among youth and the influence of television on aggressive behavior.

• *A description of the salient features of the strategic plan for achieving the district's character education strategy.* Next, students should hear a brief overview of how the district is working to help them grow as ethical, responsible citizens. They should be helped to see how the head, heart, and hand concept relates to the prosocial behavior codes of each school, their community service, the modeling that staff members present, the caring strategies of the district (such as advisory programs), and the discussions of core values that occur in classes. Without this level of student understanding, discussions of core values occur in a vacuum.

After I developed the preceding three-point context or larger picture, I met with the faculties of the two elementary schools that had already implemented Heartwood. I presented my concerns about the absence of a context for implementing Heartwood and shared my ideas for creating a larger picture for students. At that time, we were about to begin the staff development for the remaining five elementary schools that were scheduled to implement Heartwood during the coming year. The Heartwood Program was in its fourth year at the school that had originally piloted it in Mt. Lebanon and in its first year at the second school to set it in motion.

Both faculties supported the idea of creating a larger picture for Heartwood's implementation and recommended presenting it to the other five faculties during the staff development program so they could decide how they would integrate into it the program. The head, heart, and hand concept generated the most positive response, with teachers observing that it could be introduced as early as 1st grade. They also endorsed the idea of presenting elements of the larger social picture and some details of the district's character education action plans to students in a developmentally appropriate way.

To convey the importance of the character education plans, they supported a special form of presentation. One suggestion was to have all 4th graders report to the auditorium for a presentation that included junior high school or high school students who had attended that elementary school. One of the 6th grade teachers felt that a local celebrity would be an effective spokesperson if 6th grade were chosen as the year to present the social picture and action plans. Teachers suggested that presenters should give concrete examples, relevant to children's lives, of what it means to know what is right, care about what is right, and do what is right. The teachers agreed that the program should be designed in a way to convey the importance of the occasion and the information presented—students should realize that the assembly is unlike any other they have experienced at that school. After the assembly, students should return to their classrooms, where their teachers will lead them through a discussion of the three-part concept of character and other ideas presented during the assembly.

Once a school district provides a common frame of reference for its elementary students, secondary teachers can make use of it when they link the core values to subject content. As students move from the elementary level to the junior high school or middle school, the middle level should reinforce the importance of the concept of character through its orientation program or through an assembly devoted to the topic. Presenters should emphasize that students should expect to see school employees exhibiting the core values through their behaviors. Students should also understand that they share with school employees an obligation to translate the moral knowledge of the head and the emotional commitment of the heart into personal action. Without that effort of ethical integrity on the part of all, the district's commitment to moral education will be a sham. Finally, as students enter the high school, the principal and staff must also reinforce the notion of character as thinking, feeling, and acting in a manner that conveys a high priority.

Lesson 2. The Subject Areas Offer Many Opportunities for Integrating the Core Values.

While every subject area can reinforce one or more of the core values, the following topics represent important opportunities for integration.

Media Literacy. Schools write curriculums in response to societal needs. When decision makers determine that a working knowledge of government at the national, state, and local levels is critical to good citizenship, a social studies curriculum is written to provide that knowledge. When a state department of education determines that significant numbers of students are at risk of contracting AIDS, the state mandates AIDS instruction in all school curriculums. A local school decides to include safe walking practices in its elementary program because many students cross busy streets on their way to school. Since nutritional habits affect physiological and intellectual development, schools instruct students about the food they consume.

By contrast, as a society we allow the average student to consume 15,000 hours of television by graduation but fail to provide any instruction to make them critical consumers of this medium. The amount of television and other electronic media that students consume has tremendous implications for character education. Regrettably, for some students, the electronic media represent the most powerful values curriculum to which they are exposed.

I once taught a parenting class in which a mother and father described the care they took to control the television their children consumed. They related a dinner conversation where they announced to their 4-year-old daughter that her 16-year-old brother was going to have his first date that night. They asked her whether she understood the word date. She quickly assured them that she did. A date consisted of a man and woman "getting all dressed up, going out to eat and then to dance, and then going home to take off their clothes and to get into bed." The shocked parents quickly assured the child that her brother wasn't going to have that kind of date. Despite their efforts, they realized their daughter had acquired that notion of a date through unsupervised moments of television watching at their house or at a friend's.

A media literacy curriculum could offer students a chance to apply higher order thinking skills to the media in order to gain a greater measure of control over its influence on their lives. Some of the ideas schools could explore in an elementary and secondary media literacy curriculum include:

1. Discussions of the extent to which films and television represent reality. For example, sometimes television characters engage in fisticuffs for extended periods without any apparent physical consequences. In the real world, a typical brawl consists

of one blow that sends two people to the emergency room—one for a broken hand and the other for a broken jaw. Students need to understand that one blow to the temple can kill another person. They also need to ask to what extent television reflects major elements of American life and how those elements are reflected. Many Americans regularly attend churches, synagogues, and temples and strive to use their religious beliefs in decision making. How often is that dimension of our culture represented in televison programming and films?

2. Commercial television should be discussed as a business enterprise: it exists to create new markets or expand existing ones. Students at the secondary level need to explore how that fact drives programming decisions.

3. Students can sharpen their analytical skills by identifying the values inherent in programs and the logic (or absence thereof) of advertising.

4. The impact of music, film, and television on behavior. Children entering adolescence typically want increased independence and begin to challenge the authority of parents. They need to consider their capacity for independent decision making as they fall under the influence of the values represented by the media. Unlike the influence of parents, which is more open and direct, the influence of the media is subtle and insidious. Students need to understand that most parents give direction out of love; the media is a commercial enterprise that loves only the young person's wallet.

Violence as a means of conflict resolution is another aspect of the media that schools can address. A growing body of research supports the argument that the depiction of violence in the electronic media contributes to the incidence of violence in this country. As critics like Michael Medved (1992) observe, media claims that programming does not influence behavior contradict their arguments that businesses should buy advertising time in order to influence consumer behavior.

5. As early as the elementary grades, students should begin to distinguish between heroes and celebrities. The media tend to focus on the latter and disabuse viewers of their notions about the former.

The Center for Media Literacy and schools of education such as Harvard's are developing instructional materials and offering teacher seminars in media literacy (see the Resources section). We must realize that if schools do not develop our students' ability to think critically about media influence, we leave them open to the media's pervasive moral miseducation.

Religion. The influence of religion in human history offers a rich opportunity for values discussions. Unfortunately, for a variety of reasons, many schools have become extremely cautious about the inclusion of religious topics. Much of what Robert Sollod has observed about the topic of religion in college curriculums is now also true of elementary and secondary curriculums:

> The curricula that most undergraduates study do little to rectify the fact that many Americans are ignorant of religious and spiritual teachings, of their significance in the history of this and other civilizations, and of their significance in contemporary society. Omitting this major facet of human experience contributes to a continuing shallowness and imbalance in much of university life today (Sollod 1992, p. A60).

Some of the confusion about the appropriate role of religion in curriculum can be traced to the Supreme Court decisions of the 1960s. But educators should keep in mind that while the justices ruled that opening exercises of reading scripture and reciting prayer were unconstitutional, they did not prohibit teaching about religion.

Paul Vitz (1986) in *Censorship: Evidence of Bias in Our Textbooks*, reports examples of religion's having been systematically excluded from school texts. He cites an elementary social studies textbook that devotes 30 pages to the pilgrims but fails to provide any detail of their religious life. Similarly, to what extent are students aware of the spiritual basis for Martin Luther King's civil rights agenda? To provide a history of any culture without attention to its spiritual elements is to build an incomplete and intellectually dishonest picture of that culture.

Social studies is not the only area in which the place of religion will emerge as a consideration. Many schools include responsible decision making in their health programs. In one school district, a committee of teachers, parents, and administrators reviewed videotapes designed to supplement instruction about AIDS. One of the tapes contained interviews with a group of high school students who had decided to abstain from sexual intercourse. One student said that her decision reflected a fear of becoming pregnant. A young man declared that he was afraid of contracting a sexually transmitted disease. A young woman said that she wasn't ready for the psychological or emotional dimensions of sexual intercourse.

One of the committee members reviewing the film expressed dismay over the absence of religious reasons for sexual abstinence. He felt that some students in his district's health classes would make their decision on sexual abstinence on the basis of religious beliefs, yet that reason was not being validated in the classroom. He argued that as students discuss reasons for sexual decision making, a spiritual basis should be included along with others.

To exclude this spiritual basis represents less than the neutral position the Constitution requires of government on the issue of religion. Schools are wise to actively encourage students to draw on all of their intellectual and cultural resources, including their faith traditions, when they are making moral decisions.

Health. Health curriculums will continue to be the focus of values discussions even when religion is not an issue. Some educators are questioning the efficacy of the "safe sex" approach to human sexuality. Lickona argues that "safe or safer sex" programs send students a mixed message—"Don't have sex, but here is a way to do it fairly safely." He urges schools to adopt an abstinence approach to guide students to the conclusion that sexual abstinence is the only medically safe and morally responsible choice for an unmarried teenager (Lickona 1993).

Another development in human sexuality and drug education curriculums reflects concern over the efficacy of information-based programs. William Bennett cites studies demonstrating that values play a more important role than knowledge in sexual behavior (Bennett 1987).

The sexuality issue represents an important challenge to any district seeking a high level of consonance between its core values and curriculum. Responsibility will receive wide support as a core value in most districts, but the translation of that value into specific behaviors around sexuality issues will be a test of a school system's consensus-building abilities.

Conflict Resolution. Mt. Lebanon selected "the peaceful resolution of conflict" as one of its core values. Its character education strategy specified that each school must develop a prosocial behavior code based on the peaceful resolution of conflict and the other five core values. Those were important first steps in making peaceful conflict resolution part of a school's fabric, but the value would have remained a mere hope if the district had failed to provide instruction around the value. (The development of the behavior codes is described in Chapter 5). Planning for conflict resolution should include instruction that begins in the elementary grades for all students and provides staff development for all employees (Willis 1993). Several conflict resolution programs are identified in the Resources section.

These and other subject areas (science and environmental issues, computer science and illegal copying of software, history and civil disobedience, mathematics and the misuse of statistics, art and community norms) offer content possibilities that are both exciting and daunting.

Lesson 3. You Can Integrate the Values into Existing Courses *and* Write a Separate Course.

The Mt. Lebanon School District chose to integrate the core values into the existing curriculum as a means of avoiding scheduling problems and taking advantage of learning opportunities that naturally present themselves in content areas. But there are also advantages in writing an ethics program that is a separate part of the curriculum. One advantage is the prominence assigned to a content area when it stands alone and is required of all students. A second advantage is greater consistency in its implementation through a stand-alone approach as opposed to an integrated approach. Third, a separate curriculum does not eliminate the integration of core values into other courses. In fact, some would argue that a separate character education curriculum facilitates reinforcement in other content areas. Schools should not decide to integrate or segregate character education content without first discussing both approaches.

Lesson 4: Do Not Trivialize Literature When Using It as a Springboard for Discussing Values.

One of the concerns expressed among the secondary language arts teachers of the Mt. Lebanon School District was a fear that literature would be reduced to moral lessons. This concern was especially acute at the high school level, where teachers often complain about students who see literature merely as a moral tale in which the reader has "to dig to find the hidden meaning of the story."

The issue here is one of degree. Admittedly, teachers can go too far and reduce a great novel to a mere fable. Teachers need to be reassured that taking advantage of the value elements inherent in literature need not represent a radical departure from their current practices. In teaching *Great Expectations*, for example, English teachers usually ask students about the growth that Pip displays. Without doing a disservice to Dickens' literary talents, framing the question by reference to a district core value (moral courage as an illustration of integrity) seems reasonable. In fact, given his views on personal and social values, Dickens would probably applaud such an attempt to link his protagonist's development with a district's core values.

Lesson 5. Assess Your Staff Development Needs Carefully; Don't Assume Too Much.

At one level, the Heartwood Program can be implemented with minimal staff development time. Mt. Lebanon focused on helping teachers understand the structure of the program, its fundamental methodology, the materials themselves, and the resources for planning lessons and home extension activities.

Most teachers, however, have not received any formal preparation at the undergraduate or graduate level for their role as character educators. Many lack a framework that includes a history of character education in America, schools of thought on how humans develop morally, a concept of moral behavior, examples of character education programs, or specific methodologies for achieving character education objectives, or strategies for dealing with controversial topics. Although Mt. Lebanon provided staff with information about some of these matters, the evaluation of the demographer's presentation to the secondary staff revealed a need for staff development that went beyond the original Heart-wood training.

Some Final Thoughts on Curriculum

A district's decision makers must proceed carefully as they take abstract qualities like responsibility down the abstraction ladder to concrete applications in specific content areas. The curriculum must have broad community support. That can be achieved in part by obtaining community input into the curriculum development process.

Further, just as a district should develop a rationale for its role in character education, a district should present the community with sound arguments for the specifics of the character education curriculum. Explain why it is important, if not critical, for students to have media literacy skills. Have a vision of what the character education curriculum might look like eventually, determine what is possible immediately and implement that, and continue to pursue the longer-term vision by building readiness and support for the more challenging components.

5

Ethos

Throughout its planning, Mt. Lebanon's Character Education Strategy Team believed that the best opportunity for nurturing ethical, responsible behavior in students lay in the creation of a comprehensive character education program. A critical dimension of the team's view of a comprehensive program was the district's ethos:

> Character develops within a social web or environment. The nature of that environment, the messages it sends to individuals, and the behaviors it encourages and discourages are important factors to consider in character education. Clear rules of conduct, student ownership of those rules, a supportive environment, and satisfaction resulting from complying with the norms of the environment shape behavior (Leming 1993, p. 69).

If the operational norms of the district failed to reflect the core values, then any curricular emphasis on the values would represent mere lip service.

The members of the Character Education Strategy Team did not view the district's existing ethos as "bad." To the contrary, they identified many outstanding qualities. They just felt that these qualities could be extended to new levels of caring and service through a formal, systematic, character education program. They designed the action plans to take the district's ethos to new levels and to give students and staff opportunities to act on the knowledge of their heads and hearts.

Four Action Plans

Mt. Lebanon's Strategic Plan addressed the district's ethos through three strategies: character education, community service, and caring. From these three strategies, action plans for four areas emerged. The first required that each school write a prosocial behavior code for students. The second called for each building to develop a community service program. The third plan created codes of ethics for the school board and all employee groups. The fourth directed the district's three organizational levels (elementary, middle/junior high, and high school) to develop plans for creating even more caring environments.

All four plans were to reflect the district's core values. The first plan is to be implemented during the fourth year of the five-year strategic planning cycle. The last three plans have been implemented.

Plan 1. Prosocial Behavior Codes for Students

The first action plan calls for a committee of teachers, administrators, parents, and students in each school to write a behavior code based on the core values. The Character Education Strategy Team considered writing a districtwide code, but concluded that commitment to a code would be stronger if it were developed at the building level.

Before building committees begin work on the codes, a member of the original Character Education Strategy Team will review the overall character education strategy with each committee to help them see the relationship of this part of the strategy to the whole. This review will emphasize three principles the code should reflect:

1. *The Code Should Emphasize Positive Behaviors.* The plan omits the word *discipline*, because for many educators and students it connotes punishment. While consequences for negative behavior will certainly be a dimension of the codes, the focus will be prosocial behaviors, emphasizing what students are to *do* rather than what they should *not do*.

2. *Parents and Students Should Help Create the Code.* A second principle holds that parents and students should help to write the

behavior codes. Each school's PTA will be asked to select several members to serve on the committee that will write the behavior code. Parental involvement should produce a higher level of community support. The inclusion of students in the process will provide another instructional opportunity and will create a group of students who can present the code to their peers and become advocates of it.

Student and parent involvement, however, should not stop with writing the building-level codes. Teachers usually extend a building code by developing their own classroom rules. Students should participate in that process too. Just as the building code should proceed from a discussion of the core values, the classroom code should be developed similarly. Teacher and students need to consider what demonstrating "active responsibility for the welfare of others" will mean in their classroom. Once the classroom code is written, parents should be informed. One school district requires its teachers to send parents copies of their classroom behavior codes.

3. *The Code Must Be Instructive.* The codes should have an instructional orientation. After the codes are written, each building committee should present the code to students and staff in a way that explains the reasons behind each element of the code. When behavioral problems occur, the code should enable students to learn from the experience. This learning relates to two facets of moral behavior: perspective and empathy. Teachers and administrators must help offending students move from their own perspectives of an incident to those of the students or adults negatively affected by their behavior. This perspective shift should occur as a result of questioning the students rather than by pronouncing judgment.

Through questions, students can be led to describe others' points of view. The questions should then require students to describe the feelings that an aggrieved party might have as a result of a particular incident. Once students understand the harm that has been done, they should then be asked what they can do to make amends—to set things right. Students should formulate plans to carry this out.

The discussion of the incident should conclude with agreement on what the student can do to avoid this kind of behavior in

49

the future. Specifically, what strategies can the student use, or which adults can he or she call upon for assistance or direction? What will the consequences be for future incidents? Should any agreements about future conduct be formalized in written agreements?

When specific problems occur within either a school or a classroom, teachers and principals should be directed to consider whether parent involvement could be helpful in the problem-solving process. Obviously, that involvement may not be necessary in many cases, but there will be situations where parent participation is critical to any improvement in the student's behavior.

In Pennsylvania, the department of education mandated that all school districts institute Instructional Support Teams (IST), an intervention program that requires parent participation. The mandate has a classroom management element that can be satisfied by using any one of several approaches.

Mt. Lebanon saw the requirement to provide staff development in classroom management as an opportunity to begin writing its building-based prosocial behavior codes. The district selected the Cooperative Discipline Program (Albert 1989) because it reflected the three principles of the action plan outlined earlier. A consultant from the Albert Program came to the district for a two-day workshop that the trainer customized to accommodate the requirements of the IST program and to integrate the district's core values.

Plan 2. Codes of Ethics for Employees and School Board

This action plan reflects the belief that character education programs must extend beyond the curriculum to all facets of a school district's operation. Adults have the responsibility and opportunity to model behaviors that will create an ethos that exemplifies a district's core values. This plan also has the potential to upset staff who point out that their job descriptions do not specify modeling the core values for students.

The action plan requires the school board and every other adult segment of the school community to adopt, publish, disseminate, and display the code of ethics, reflecting the core values, that it expects its members to follow. The process began when the school board and each employee group recruited a

member to serve on the Code of Ethics Action Plan Implementation Team. The cafeteria workers were the only group that could
not find a volunteer to serve on the district committee.

Once organized, the team began its work by reviewing the
codes of ethics of educational associations and unions, manufac-
turing and service enterprises, and school board associations.
After reviewing these codes, members of the committee wrote the
five principles that each regarded as most important for a district
code. Because there were areas of agreement among the seven
committee members, the activity produced 16 different ideas.

The final version of the code contained the district's mission
statement,the six core values, and nine principles of conduct for
employees and the school board.

Code of Ethics

Mission

The mission of Mt. Lebanon School District, as the leader of
an educational partnership with the community, is to ensure
that all students acquire the knowledge and skills to succeed
and contribute as ethical, responsible citizens in a rapidly
changing global society through a challenging comprehensive program taught in a safe, caring environment by an
exceptional staff with continued involvement of families.

In order for the District to fulfill this mission, especially nurturing the
development of ethical, responsible behavior in its students, the staff and
members of the Board of School Directors will seek to model the
District's Core Values in their work.

Core Values

These core values are a statement of belief of the Mt. Lebanon School
District.

We believe that the morally mature person habitually:

1. Respects human dignity
2. Demonstrates active responsibility for the welfare of others
3. Integrates individual interests and social responsibilities
4. Demonstrates integrity
5. Applies moral principles when making choices and judgments
6. Seeks peaceful resolution of conflict

The Mt. Lebanon School District Code of Ethics lists the principles of conduct which the staff and Board of School Directors are expected to follow.

As members of the school community, we should seek to:

1. Promote the well-being, interests, and needs of students through our decisions and our actions.

2. Treat others fairly and respectfully, recognize their right to hold individual views, and seek to understand those views.

3. Maintain the confidentiality of information obtained in the course of duty, unless disclosure is required by law or is shared on a "need to know" basis in the best interests of individuals.

4. Respect and cooperate with families and community groups which have an important role in the nurturing and development of students.

5. Use the District's time and material resources for intended purposes, refrain from misusing our positions for personal gain, and avoid being placed in a position of conflict of interest.

6. Act in a responsible and professional manner, and seek to extend our professional knowledge and skills.

7. Perform our duties with pride and to the best of our abilities.

8. Maintain our physical and mental well-being and display a positive and open attitude.

9. Abide by all District policies and procedures.

The school board and each employee group have adopted the Code of Ethics. Laminated copies are being prepared for all employees to display in a prominent place at their work sites.

The Character Education Strategy Team that wrote the Code of Ethics Action Plan wrestled with the question of the consequences of code violations. Should violations lead to censure by the employee's group? Should or could the district take action against the employee? How would the school board handle a code violation by one of its own members? After much discussion, the team decided to pass on the issue of code violations for two reasons. First, they wanted employees to focus on the code as a guide for modeling the core values through the nine principles rather than as a means of calling them to account for violations. Second, extreme cases of inappropriate behavior probably represented a violation of law, school district policy, or district procedures and would be addressed through progressive discipline or legal charges reflecting one or more of those sources.

The Code of Ethics Action Plan requires that the school board and each employee group review the code at the end of the first year and revise it if necessary. Thereafter, the code will be reviewed at least once every three years.

Plan 3. Community Service for All Schools

The Strategic Planning Team of the Mt. Lebanon School District regarded community service as such an important undertaking that the team devoted an entire strategy to it rather than simply include it in the character education strategy. The original action plans for the strategy require the elementary and junior high schools to develop building-level projects while giving individual grade levels or classrooms the option of undertaking community service. At the high school level, 120 hours of community service were mandated for high school graduation.

The committee responsible for developing the elementary portion of the strategy developed a position paper that significantly influenced the development of the program at the elementary and secondary levels. The most important component of the elementary position paper called for the inclusion of a learning component. Service without the opportunity for structured learning and reflection struck the members of the elementary committee as inadequate. They described the following essential elements of community service:

1. It must be meaningful. The participants must have a sense of ownership or importance.

2. It should have an end product. From the outset of the project, participants and service recipients alike must have a clear sense of (a) what is to be accomplished and (b) what is to be learned. Attention to the important factor of mutuality in the service learning exchange protects the service from becoming patronizing charity.

3. Participants must have a preplanned opportunity for reflection: *Why did we do this? How did you feel about this? Let's think about what we did.*

4. Participants should be thanked and should be made aware of outcomes.

5. It should be developmentally appropriate.

With the publication of the elementary position paper, the district began to describe its program as *Service Learning* rather than Community Service. The junior high school and high school Service Learning Implementation Teams began to design programs that focused on learning and included an opportunity for students to reflect on the experience under the direction of a trained adult facilitator.

Like the elementary schools, the junior high school was under no mandate to have students complete a designated number of service hours. Students had the opportunity to participate in a variety of classroom and school projects, such as the school's annual muscular dystrophy fundraising drive.

All three levels of the system recognized that service should not be limited to organizations outside of the school district. Service to adults and other students within the building was recognized as an acceptable means of participating in service learning. Given the challenge of providing for the safety of young children, service within the building may be the only manageable approach for some elementary schools.

At the high school level, the requirement that students complete 120 hours of service learning before graduation became a concern for several school directors. Some objected to the number of hours and others to required participation. The latter group was concerned about a legal challenge to the community service graduation requirement of Liberty High School in Bethlehem, Pennsylvania. Subsequent to the board's discussion, the U.S. Supreme Court refused to review a lower federal court's decision to uphold the graduation requirement. The Mt. Lebanon School Board, however, eventually decided to abandon the graduation requirement.

Plan 4. Caring Environments in All Schools

This strategy reflected a growing consensus in the field of character education that schools must be caring communities if they wish to nurture their students' full human development. For example, the Child Development Project seeks to build supportive adult-child relationships through an ethic of caring: "We believe that children are inclined to emulate adults with whom they have positive relationships and to reciprocate the ways they are treated, and thus we try to help parents and teachers to form warm and supportive relationships with children" (Watson et al. 1989, p. 56). In Mt. Lebanon, each level in the school system reflected on how its organization and practices contributed to the creation of a caring environment.

The Elementary Caring Implementation Team decided to focus on identifying the characteristics of each age as a means of helping teachers and administrators evaluate the developmental appropriateness of instructional practices. Teachers, administrators, and educators and mental health specialists from the community wrote the papers that became the basis for the review process. The kindergarten teachers in the district's seven elementary schools have used the material to review the philosophy of their curriculum. Many children entering kindergarten in the district come from nursery schools that emphasize preparation for reading and other academic skills. By contrast, the district's kindergarten program reflected the thinking of Elkind (1981) and others who have urged schools to resist the trend toward pushing academic content to lower grades at the expense of social development.

The junior high school, an award-winning school with a strong academic orientation, decided to study practices typically associated with middle schools. After more than a year of study and school visits, a study committee recommended the implementation of three practices: interdisciplinary teaching teams, a mentoring program, and an exploratory program.

The junior high school staff saw teaming as a means of creating a school-within-a-school and realizing improved learning through interdisciplinary opportunities that are often missed in departmentally organized curriculums. Daily team meetings will provide teachers with a collective view of individual student needs.

Mentoring will provide an opportunity for students to have regular contact with an adult who can help them with topics that often are not included in a school's curriculum. Homeroom advisory groups, for example, will assure 7th graders entering the junior high school that their feelings of anxiety about leaving a smaller elementary school are normal and that a group of caring adults and 8th graders are committed to making their transition as smooth as possible.

The exploratory program seeks to capitalize on the early adolescent's natural curiosity and to provide short-term learning opportunities outside of the curriculum. If the development of an exploratory program follows that of many other middle schools, the offerings will probably grow out of staff hobbies and interests and will provide students a chance to see other dimensions of the faculty and administration.

The adoption of middle school practices that have been used for decades by no means represents a revolutionary move by a school district. What makes the approach of the Mt. Lebanon School District somewhat different is the use of these practices to help create an ethos of caring. Just as interdisciplinary teaming provides an opportunity for learners to see relationships among art, philosophy, science, literature, politics, and religion, the ethos strategies of the Mt. Lebanon Junior High School give students, parents, and staff an opportunity to make new and conscious connections among a variety of instructional practices designed to nurture caring, ethical, and responsible behavior.

The high school adopted several practices designed to create a more caring environment. Certainly, service learning contributes to an ethos of caring. Another plan called for identifying a group of twenty 9th graders who were not identified as leaders by their teachers but who had the potential to grow as leaders if given the right opportunity. These students were invited to participate in a leadership training program sponsored by the University of Pittsburgh the summer before their sophomore year. The program, called MAPS (Maximizing Adolescent Potential in Students), involved an intense week of training by the MAPS staff and several Mt. Lebanon teachers. The students then shared their experiences with a group of teachers and administrators at a graduation luncheon. The growth described by the students and MAPS staff was remarkable. Students described increased self-confidence in working with students they hadn't known before and a greater willingness to risk leadership behaviors.

During the school year, the Mt. Lebanon teachers who participated in the MAPS training provided follow-up support to further nurture the students' growth. In the program's second year, two groups of 20 students received the summer MAPS training. The junior high school is investigating the creation of a middle-level version of the program.

Some members of the high school staff are discussing the application of selected middle school practices to the high school. Interdisciplinary teaching teams at 9th grade are being considered as a means of facilitating the transition from junior high to high school. On the other hand, a significant number of high school teachers have expressed concern over implementing a mentoring program for all students, as the junior high school has done. Some teachers believe the effort will not be as effective with high school students. Others believe they have not been prepared for a role that they essentially see as counseling.

A consultant to the district has suggested that the principal seek faculty volunteers for mentoring roles and then establish advisory groups for a portion of the student body. To augment the school's Student Assistance Program, mentoring groups could be formed around such topics as peer pressure.

Another approach to creating mentoring groups involves having the staff identify students who quietly and inconspicuously pass through the school without ever drawing attention. Without assuming that these students have problems, the staff would invite them to join mentoring groups as a way to encourage them to meet new students and work with a caring adult.

Creating a caring ethos does not depend solely on new "programs." The high school principal has made a commitment to seeing every student group and team perform at least once during the year. Through his faculty advisory council, he encourages teachers to attend student performances. He also walks across the street to visit with the students who smoke and often dress in black. The modeling provided by the principal is an essential element of a caring environment.

Lessons Learned

Lesson 1. Design Programs for Classified (Noncertificated) Employees.

A school district desiring to involve classified employees in creating an ethos based on the district's core values must make plans that go beyond just informing them of the program. Our mistake was to deny classified employees the same opportunities to participate in implementing action plans that we gave to teachers, administrators, and parents. For example, the action plan for writing building-level prosocial behavior codes specified that teachers, administrators, parents, and students should write the codes. No representation, however, from the classified group was mandated by the plan—a serious oversight that conveyed an unfortunate message.

After the initial overview of the district's character education strategy for all employees, the district should have undertaken a program to build further awareness of the issues and opportunities for the classified staff. We should have given further consideration to recommendations growing out of the Lickona meeting with the classified employees, by taking such actions as implementing the cafeteria workers' suggestion that they be issued name tags. Through homerooms and Student Council, we should have pursued the goal of increasing student sensitivity, focusing on their remarks about the quality of the cafeteria's food. We could also have developed training sessions on modeling behaviors that reflect the core values for each classified employee group. These are just some of the ideas a district should consider if it is serious about bringing all employees into a character education effort.

Lesson 2. Be Clear About the Goals for Service Learning or Community Service.

Service learning can become an emotional issue. Districts should consider two factors in establishing goals for the program. First, what is the desired outcome of the undertaking? Some schools believe that the goal of nurturing a spirit or atmosphere of altruism is sufficient and are content to have students and service recipients feel good about the experience. While that is a commendable goal, it doesn't realize the potential that service learning provides. Limiting community service to the creation of an altruistic atmosphere focuses on the heart and hand portions of the concept of the moral person. Schools should also establish instructional goals that speak to the head.

Under the direction of a trained facilitator, students can learn from their experiences. For example, in working with the elderly, students should learn about government policy and social attitudes toward the aged and gain insight into the views of a generation with whom many students have limited contact. Students could be asked to identify two or three needs of the group they are serving or to describe how the needs of the elderly who live at home alone are both similar to and different from those who are living in nursing homes.

If, then, a school district chooses to specify the learning outcomes it wants students to achieve through the experience, the issue of a clock hour requirement should become moot. That is, successful completion of a service learning program should consist of providing evidence that the instructional objectives have been met, not that hours have been "served."

Second, whether a district selects the outcomes or clock-hour route, it must decide whether the program will be mandatory or voluntary. Recognizing strong arguments on both sides of the issue, I urge schools to consider a mandatory program. My position reflects a commitment to providing students with a head, heart, and hand concept of the moral person.

Many students will not experience the joy and knowledge that service to others can provide if the decision to participate is voluntary. Most people can remember an instance when social pressure or a parental mandate forced them to do something for another. In such an experience, initial resentment and anger are often transformed into insight and pleasure. Mandatory service learning offers the opportunity for actions of the hand to transform the heart and and educate the head.

Similarly, voluntary community service will deny many students the opportunity to develop the self-discipline and knowledge required for this form of altruistic behavior. William Kilpatrick cites Aristotle's belief that virtues are developed by understanding and practicing them:

If Aristotle was right about this, it means, of course, that much of our modern talk about "choices" and decision making" is rather shallow. An individual can't choose to do something if he lacks the capacity for it. For example, running the Boston Marathon is not a choice for those who are out of shape. In a similar fashion, a child's freedom to choose altruistic behavior over self-centered behavior is severely limited if he has never formed a habit of helping others in need. Far from stifling our freedom to chose, habits actually enhance it. They give us command and control of ourselves (Kilpatrick 1992, pp. 97–98).

Lesson 3. Make Manners and Sportsmanship Part of the Ethos Discussion.

The development and implementation of prosocial behavior codes provide an excellent opportunity for discussions of manners or social conventions. Manners is a word that has virtually disappeared from many discussions of behavior. Any consideration of manners should distinguish between what Nucci refers to as morality and societal convention:

Conventions are arbitrary because there is nothing inherently right or wrong about the actions they define; for example, children could just as easily refer to their teachers by first names as by titles of Mr. or Mrs. Through accepted usage, however, these standards serve to coordinate the interactions of individuals within social systems by providing them with a set of expectations regarding appropriate behavior (Nucci 1989, p. 184).

Students can learn about different social groups and cultures by examining social conventions. The ubiquitous baseball cap offers an opportunity to discuss how conventions change or remain the same depending on the setting. Some schools allow students to wear hats inside the school, including classrooms. Others do not. In some religious settings, males must wear something on their head; in other religious settings, a hat would violate an important convention. Students should learn to distinguish between conventions and values that are universal because of an intrinsic factor (e.g., hitting another is wrong because it will harm the victim).

Distinctions between manners and universal values will sometimes blur, and profanity offers an illustration of how that can occur. Any school committee writing a behavior code should consider the question of acceptable language. Profanity will be part of the vocabulary that some students bring to school because their parents may permit them to use it at home. But profanity can offend some people, and our awareness of that fact carries an obligation to avoid it. That position suggests a moral dimension for this aspect of manners.

Manners can be viewed as one way of demonstrating the self-control and sensitivity that symbolize civilized behavior. Tony Jarns, headmaster of Roxbury Latin School in Boston, opened the 1990 school year with these remarks to the student body and staff:

> Manners are the most rudimentary way in which we acknowledge the existence of others in the world, in which we curb our natural selfish instincts. . . . That is what manners are: the mundane basic recognition that others exist and have as much right to their place on earth as we do. Manners are the fundamental curbings and limitings of our own self-expression (Jarns 1990).

Instruction in manners can complement a district's effort to help students develop peaceful means of resolving conflict. As Jarns has observed, manners provide an opportunity to "curb our natural selfish instincts." If students can begin to develop some measure of impulse control in tranquil social settings, then they might possibly learn to transfer some of that impulse control to more volatile conflict situations.

If the 1980s were a period of narcissism, nowhere was that more apparent than in sports, as the media depicted one sports hero after another displaying tantrums and rude behavior. Good sportsmanship holds that one does not taunt an opponent, that one's celebration of achievement should consider the feelings of the opponent, that spontaneous expressions of joy are less offensive than planned, choreographed ones, and that accolades should come from others rather than oneself.

Athletics offer a wonderful opportunity for putting core values into practice. Comprehensive character education efforts will include action plans for athletics. For some coaches that will lead to dilemmas, as their values clash with the core values of the

61

school system. Most coaches, however, will welcome such plans as a validation of what they have taught for years.

Lesson 4. District Recruitment, Employee Evaluation, and Inservice Education Programs Must Support the Character Education Strategy.

Recruitment brochures and the employment application should contain the district's mission statement and core values. In the interview process, interviewers should probe applicants' views of their responsibility for modeling behaviors. Teacher and administrator applicants should answer questions about their knowledge of moral development, their commitment to school involvement in that process, and their understanding of character education methodologies.

Typically, a district's noncertificated or classified staff will have been hired without having been told that they have responsibilities for modeling certain kinds of behaviors for students. The interviewer will ask a custodian applicant about the proper use of powerful cleaning agents but rarely will explore the candidate's view of conflict resolution.

Applicants for custodial positions should be asked questions about how they interact with children. They should be queried about what they would do if they encountered a student in tears in the hall. The interviewer should focus on evidence of sensitivity and good judgment rather than on specific actions or steps. The desired specific actions should then become the goal of new employee orientation and ongoing staff development. Once hired, all employees should have induction or orientation programs that present the district's character education program and the individual employee's responsibilities for that program.

Finally, if the district wants to convey the importance of this dimension, it will ensure that the employee evaluation system assesses the employee's work in this area. The evaluation system should identify the behaviors it wants employees to manifest as they carry out their character education responsibilities. Certainly "caring" behaviors are harder to describe and evaluate than the steps necessary for the safe preparation of food or the steps that a teacher might follow in teaching process writing. Nevertheless, the challenge should not deter districts from identifying appropriate and inappropriate behaviors in employees' relationships with students and colleagues.

In Mt. Lebanon, a committee of teachers and administrators developed an observation resource guide for their teacher evaluation system that described teacher interactions at three levels: preferred, appropriate, and inappropriate. A similar approach could be used with evaluation systems for other employees.

Why *Ethos?*

As I thought about a title for this chapter, I was concerned about using the term *ethos*, a word that some readers might regard as pretentious or ethereal. Reflecting on the ideas presented in this chapter, I realized that the idea of influencing our district's ethos through the character education strategy was never a stated goal of our planning. At no point during the planning process did I hear a member of the Strategic Planning Team or any Strategy or Action Plan Implementation Team use the word *ethos.*

We did, however, recognize that our program would have to be comprehensive in order to achieve the kind of influence we sought. Our goal of writing a comprehensive character education program probably reflected a subconscious or unstated recognition that our action plans were designed to achieve something larger than the sum of the plans.

That observation prompts me to ask what we would have gained had we initially declared that we sought to influence the school system's ethos through our character education strategy. At the very least, we probably would have asked if our overall plan was sufficiently comprehensive. Our answers to those questions during the planning stage possibly would have helped us recognize gaps in some plans, such as the absence of students as an audience in our Communication Action Plan or our failure to plan follow-up staff development for classified employees.

If nothing else, a discussion of a district's ethos will probably help people clarify their expectations for a character education program. Can a program that fails to positively influence a district's ethos ever be regarded as successful?

6

Parent Education

Mt. Lebanon's view of a comprehensive character education program included active parental involvement. In addition to including parents in selecting the district's core values and creating building-based prosocial behavior codes, our character education strategy called for developing programs to help parents with their role as their child's primary moral educator.

The action plan, however, specified that the character education programs for parents be funded through self-supporting fees or grants from outside agencies. This funding decision reflected the Character Education Strategy Team's belief that the district's resources should be allocated for *direct* service to students. In a district where fewer than 25 percent of the households had children enrolled in the public schools, any decision to expand services to parents by using tax dollars risked community opposition based on a position that the district's mission was to educate children, not parents.

It is worth noting, however, that the Character Education Strategy Team's view on this issue did not reflect the actual district practice. At the junior high school, for example, a counselor had provided the Step Teen Parenting series on school time for more than a decade. The program was so successful that he had a waiting list for the series, and the program had never been attacked as an inappropriate undertaking for the school district. Nevertheless, on the funding of character education parenting programs, the Character Education Strategy Team's view prevailed when the district's Strategic Planning Team accepted the plan without change.

The Parent Education Action Plan specified that parenting seminars be a continuing effort. The seminars were to run from 8 to 12 weeks and were to be offered at five levels, for parents of (1) preschoolers, (2) primary age children, (3) intermediate grade children, (4) middle-level students, and (5) high school students. Further, the team wanted the series to reflect an integrative approach to character education, specifically that described by Tom Lickona in *Raising Good Children*. Lickona's approach combined stage development and behaviorist theory and research.

The district established partnerships with two local mental health agencies to write and deliver character education parenting programs. The funding for one came from a legislative grant while the second was funded by a local health care foundation. Both agencies followed the original plan (series offered at five developmental levels) and did variations on that approach. Series have consisted of both six and eight sessions. The consistent element in all approaches has been the inclusion of the district's core values. All programs have emphasized the need for the school and family to form a partnership to nurture the development of ethical, responsible student behavior.

After two years, only one agency, the Parent and Child Guidance Center, appears ready to continue delivering the parent education programs. The format they envision for the long-term reflects what they have learned during the initial two years of the effort:

• Future series will be offered at two levels rather than five—for parents of preschool-through-elementary-age children and for parents of secondary-age students—because the number of participants did not warrant five levels.

• Second, the preschool through elementary level continues to attract three and four times the number of secondary school parents. The numbers for the former group are large enough to offer one preschool through elementary section during the school day and another during the evening.

• Future series will consist of six sessions. This appears to be the longest term that most parents will commit to attending. Offered each fall, this series will present the basic parenting infor-

65

mation that has been part of each earlier series. This content includes the stages of moral development (Lickona 1983), the district's six core values, skills and strategies for helping children recognize and adopt values, and Bruce Baldwin's seven parenting keys (Baldwin 1988).

• The spring term will be devoted to single topics that extend the subjects introduced in the fall series. These topics will be presented in a one-, two-, or three-evening format. Although the spring topics will be extensions of the fall series, participation in the fall series will not be a prerequisite for the spring series. The single-topic programs will probably include the father's role in moral development; media literacy; the acquisition of values; and management and discipline.

Although the Parenting Action Plan did not call for the creation of a character education resource center, the district decided to create one for the use of staff and parents. For parents, the materials include audiotapes and videotapes, books, articles, and a complete set of the Heartwood elementary and junior high school materials. The availability of these materials has been advertised through the PTA and the character education parenting programs. Administrators are considering additional ways of informing parents of the availability of materials.

Lessons Learned

Lesson 1. Establish Parameters for the District's Role as a Social Agency.

School districts are under increasing pressure to expand their services. For Mt. Lebanon, state and federal legislation has produced new mandates in areas such as special education, girls' athletics, programs for gifted students, student assistance teams, and curriculums for computer technology, drugs and alcohol, and AIDS. In addition to these state and federal mandates, schools in many communities are being asked to become the institution of last resort for some children. Breakfast and lunch programs, latchkey programs, preschool and full-day kindergartens are some of the services that districts are being asked to provide. Some school boards are reluctant to expand their mission to include support that has historically been provided by the family and other agencies.

While character education has historically been part of the schools' mission, providing support services such as parenting seminars has not. Schools that are considering character education should determine what role parents will play as (1) participants in planning and (2) clients of services. With respect to the former, parental involvement in writing a character education plan, developing a set of core values, and writing prosocial behavior codes should be a given. Without this participation, a district's character education program will be at risk because it lacks representative parent ownership.

The more difficult question is whether a district should develop action plans designed to support parents in their role as the primary character educator. This form of support will go beyond what many school districts view as their mission. If a district aspires to create a truly comprehensive character education program, however, support services for parents are integral.

Lesson 2. Consider Creative Ways of Funding Character Education Programs for Parents.

Parental support need not cost a lot of money. The decision of the Mt. Lebanon Character Education Strategy Team to have the parenting series funded through fees or grants represents a possible model for other districts. Programs such as parenting seminars can be offered with no or minimal expense to local taxpayers if the district brokers rather than funds or delivers the service. Some mental health agencies have the resources necessary to offer ongoing parenting seminars. Government and foundation grants are other possibilities for supporting programs. School districts historically have not been as inclined to seek funding from these sources as have their college and university cousins.

Other creative approaches to support programs can work. Borrowing from the legal profession's practice of pro bono work, an elementary school psychologist and a psychologist from a local mental health agency donated their lunch hour once a week to work with a fairly large number of 6th graders in one school who were experiencing problems because of their parents' recent divorce or separation. Of course, this occurred only after obtaining parental permission.

The leadership training that Mt. Lebanon provides sophomores during the summer as part of its caring strategy was funded for the first year by a Drug-Free Schools state grant and during years two and three by a grant from a local foundation. At the end of the third year, enough staff members had been trained through the initial grants that the continuing cost of the program had dropped to $1,500 per year. The principal convinced several local businesses to become the patrons for the ongoing cost of this leadership training.

Teachers represent a powerful source of support for character education. The local teachers' union, recognizing an opportunity to model the core value "demonstrates active responsibility for the welfare of others," has initiated its own community service program. In addition to the collective action of the union, individual teachers have become involved in community service activities.

Lesson 3. Effective Parent Support Requires a Multifaceted Approach.

Mt. Lebanon's character education parenting partnership with the local mental health agencies provided an important service to a group of parents committed to extending their skills in this important area. The agencies experimented with several formats as they tried to reach the largest number of parents possible. They finally decided to present a six-part series devoted to several critical elements of character education along with single-topic programs of one to three sessions.

The parents who have participated in the character education seminars appear to be fairly effective parents already. At times, the seminar leaders felt as though they were "preaching to the choir." The district's leaders have given considerable thought to how they can reach other parents who can't commit to six sessions or aren't attracted by the "packaging" of the program. A number of additional possibilities exist for schools wanting to provide a variety of parenting support programs.

One way of reaching parents who work outside the home is through employer-supported "brown bag" lunches. Once a week an employer provides the setting (and in some cases the lunch and cost of the instruction) for an agency to provide a character education parenting series. The same arrangement can be used for occasional single-topic programs that require just one to three lunchtimes, which might be the best way to explore employee interest in lunchtime personal development sessions.

School sponsorship of family activities can provide instruction as well as entertainment. Film Nights for families have been an important component of the Child Development Project (Murphy 1988). One way to present a Film Night is to invite families to view a movie (complete with refreshments). After the film, parents and children break into small groups in which a facilitator leads a discussion of the film's values.

This activity can have several benefits. First, it provides an opportunity for parents and children to have an evening out together. Second, the experience can help participants become more critical consumers of the media and understand its potential to influence the development of values. Third, the facilitator models discussion skills parents can use with their children when they view other movies and television shows together. Again, the cost of this type of programming can be minimal. Parent-teacher organizations often will sponsor such events.

Many cable television operators have contracts that require them to provide services to the municipality with whom they have the contract. These services often include providing equipment or access to equipment that allows the municipality to create its own local programming. In Mt. Lebanon, the cable company provides both technical support and a channel dedicated to school use. The district is just beginning to use the channel and is considering the kinds of programs that it might air.

For parents who can't attend parenting seminars outside of the home, the cable channel offers the opportunity to deliver instruction to the home. With the use of a telephone, the program can be interactive. The school district has already worked with the local medical society to offer an interactive "House Calls" medical program. Local mental health or other social agencies would probably welcome the opportunity to provide parenting seminars over a cable system.

Returning to an important point from Chapter 4, literature remains a natural opportunity for adults and children to discuss values. Teachers could offer parents instruction on using literature for family entertainment and values discussions. This resource could be offered in the schools and over a cable system.

School districts must make a policy decision about their role in family support. That decision should reflect philosophy, not economics. Mt. Lebanon and other schools have shown that districts can both broker and deliver family support programs at minimal cost if the staff is allowed to use its creativity.

7

Evaluation

E valuation poses one of the larger challenges facing any school district seeking to implement a character education program. Opponents of character education often express their concerns through rhetorical questions about evaluation. The most common questions are those regarding how to measure the effects of character education programs and how to evaluate individual students: *What evidence do you have that Program X works? How will my child be graded? What if my child fails to give the "politically correct" answer?* For many, the questions are not rhetorical but genuine attempts to seek information. In Mt. Lebanon we have experienced all of these concerns and questions.

Initially, evaluation did not play a major role in the district's character education planning. For example, Mt. Lebanon's Strategic Planning Team did not review the literature on the effects of specific programs before including character education in its strategic plan. Even if the team had reviewed such studies, without spending considerable time and obtaining assistance from a researcher, they may still have had questions about what confidence they could place in the findings.

For example, the Hartshorne and May studies conducted from 1928 to 1930 concluded that current programs probably did little good and possibly some harm. The same studies, however, also found that some classrooms in the same building were significantly more honest than others—a difference that the researchers attributed to the moral climate created by the teacher (Hartshorne and May 1928–1930). James Leming (1993) provides an excellent synthesis of character education research.

In assessing the meaning of those findings, we need to determine the nature of the programs that were being studied. Were they one-dimensional, didactic approaches or comprehensive programs similar to the Child Development Project? My reading of character education practices from the period studied by Hartshorne and May suggests the former prevailed as practice.

The strategic planning model used by the district required all of the Strategy Teams to include evaluation components in their action plans. The Character Education Strategy Team specified two kinds of evaluations in most of their action plans: implementation and outcome assessments. Implementation assessment seeks to determine to what extent a program has in fact been implemented; for example, does its operation reflect what is called for in the written plan? Outcome assessment provides information about the effects of the program: to what extent have its goals been met?

Although each of the character education action plans called for evaluations, most plans provided just general direction for assessment activities. For example, from the action plan for parent education:

> Course attendees should complete a course evaluation at the
> end of each course. (Purpose: to identify strong points and
> areas requiring improvements.)

The implementation teams for this and the other character education action plans were left to develop similar statements into specific assessment activities. Fortunately, the Parenting Action Plan was funded by a foundation that required a third-party evaluation, the cost of which was included in the grant. The evaluations were conducted by the educational arm of the St. Francis Health System, a local hospital that had considerable experience evaluating the effects of drug and alcohol programs. The St. Francis evaluators focused on parental knowledge, attitudes, and practices and the parents' satisfaction with the program's structure. During the course itself, parents took pre- and post-tests on content. Six months after the course, structured telephone interviews sought to determine what effect the experience had on parenting behavior related to character education. Those reports are forthcoming.

The pre- and post-tests for the preschool through elementary parenting series and all but one of the single-topic programs indicated "significant increases in knowledge gained." The series for parents of secondary students and the family values single-topic program did not produce significant increases. The follow-up surveys of parents indicated "a significant change in beliefs between the time the parent entered the training and the follow-up period (six months)." We are considering the evaluation findings and their implications for future programming. For example, the results of the secondary parent series may have reflected erratic attendance among a group that was small from the outset. The junior high school principal believes that a more ambitious publicity program will increase parent participation and has included information about the secondary series in his opening-of-school newsletter and presentations to the PTA. The agency delivering the series reports that registration for the fall 1994 series was 20, an increase of 16. This increase also reinforces a point made earlier: that is, the need for principals to be visible champions of character education in their buildings.

The Character Education Curriculum Action Plan identified several evaluation needs and issues. The first need was to select a character education program from among those being reviewed by the team. The Curriculum Action Plan Implementation Team reviewed the evaluation data available for each of the programs.

At the elementary level, Heartwood had the inside track throughout the process because it was being piloted in one of the district's elementary schools. The reader may recall from Chapter 4 that the Heartwood pilot occurred independent of the district's character education initiative; that is, the building principal received permission to pilot the program a year before the district had developed a strategic plan and a character education strategy. Furthermore, the Curriculum Implementation Action Team not only had an opportunity to collect data from one of their elementary schools but also from a pilot of Heartwood in 79 classrooms in 7 Pittsburgh elementary schools and in 15 Pennsylvania suburban, urban, and rural districts.

The critical element in the data from all of the Heartwood pilots was teachers' perception of the program. Using a scale of 1 (strongly disagree) to 4 (strongly agree), 11 of 17 teachers in the

Mt. Lebanon pilot strongly agreed that "This program is an effective tool for exposing students to issues of ethics." Five others assigned it a value of 3.

The City of Pittsburgh evaluation reported "changes in nature of classroom discussion, increased atmosphere of caring and sharing." Pittsburgh's teachers and administrators strongly recommended the continuation of the program (Piscolish 1991). For the Pennsylvania study, investigators from Research for Better Schools found:

> Almost all teachers emphasized the importance and need for this type of program in their schools. Teachers felt strongly that students were lacking in their ethical development, and that this program provided a constructive strategy for initiating discussions with students in this critical area (Buttram et al. 1992, p. 5).

Another evaluation issue arose when a member of the Mt. Lebanon school board questioned the wisdom of piloting the junior high school version of Heartwood, for which there were no evaluative data. Citing the competence of our staff, I pointed out that the program had been developed collaboratively by the district's English department and Heartwood. I emphasized that the program was an extension of a curriculum that already enjoyed positive faculty and parent support in two of our elementary schools. (At the time of the question, Heartwood was being implemented in a second district school.) I argued that exploring values through literature was a regular and natural part of language arts instruction. What was different, however, was the selection of literature that allowed teachers to connect stories to the district's core values. Further, like the elementary program, the junior high school version would include home extension activities designed to inform parents and involve them as partners in the process.

The discussion of the junior high school version of Heartwood was important for two reasons. First, it brought to the surface important issues regarding evaluation. We began to respond to the questions and concerns with written positions. Some of those are included in the "Lessons Learned" portion of this chapter. Second, it was a test of the board's continuing support for character education. Since the adoption of the district's strategic plan in 1991, six of the nine school board members who had approved the original plan had left the board. We realized that we needed to include information about our character education initiative in orientation sessions for new board members.

After responding to the questions at the school board meeting, I wrote a follow-up memo elaborating the points I had presented orally. This memo provided the new board members with an important character education background.

Lessons Learned

Lesson 1. Design the Evaluation Component During the Initial Planning Process.

Too often schools think about program evaluation during or after implementation or do not invest enough time during the planning stage of program development. Evaluation design should occur during the planning stage by determining the evaluation questions that need to be answered. Evaluation needs will probably cluster around three assessment areas:

• Implementation—Was the program implemented as planned?

• Program—What were the results of the program?

• Student—How will individual students be evaluated? Planners should consider undertaking all three types of evaluation.

As a district communicates the details of its character education strategy to the community and staff, it should describe all of the evaluation components in its plan. Addressing program and student evaluation in these early communications will demonstrate that the planners considered parent concerns.

As the evaluation component is developed, a planning team will need to determine the questions they want answered. Certainly evaluation should seek to determine the extent to which a program's goals have been achieved. One of the advantages of developing an evaluation component early in the process is the probability that the discussions will produce important refinements of the goals. As people seek ways to measure a program's goals, they sometimes will pause and ask if the goal as stated actually reflects what they want. In other situations, they find that the goal is too amorphous to assess.

Another reason for early attention to evaluation is the need to identify any baseline data that will be used. Schools often will need to collect pre-implementation data in order to measure the effects of a program. For example, if a program seeks to reduce the number of student altercations through a conflict resolution curriculum, the staff will need to identify the kinds of data they will collect to measure results—such as school suspensions for fighting, teacher perceptions, student self-reports. Having identified those, does the school have or can staff obtain information about the pre-implementation levels for those indicators?

Lesson 2. Review the Literature on the Evaluation of Character Education Early in the Process.

It is important for those involved in planning character education to know something of the history of character education evaluation and research for several reasons. First, a review of that history will produce knowledge that will allow planners to proactively address important questions about student evaluation and grading and the success of various programs. Some critics will cite research that questions the efficacy of character education. Others will wonder whether character education outcomes can even be assessed. After all, classrooms are not sterile laboratories where teachers can control the variables influencing the development of values. For example, a school's well-designed program for nurturing respect may fail to produce growth in a child who daily returns home to a family that regularly models disrespect.

School leaders need to understand character education research and be able to cite findings that report positive outcomes. There is a growing body of positive findings about the results of programs. For example, the Child Development Project is a character education program that provided Mt. Lebanon's Character Education Strategy Team with important ideas about what a comprehensive program should offer. Four aspects of the Project had particular appeal for us:

• A literature-based approach to reading and language arts that encourages children to think deeply, complexly, and appreciatively about what they read, while helping them build empathy for others and values such as loyalty and caring;

• A cooperative approach to classroom learning that emphasizes the importance of challenging and meaningful learning tasks, the benefits of collaborating on learning tasks, and the importance of learning to work with others in fair, caring, and responsible ways;

• An approach to classroom management and discipline that builds a caring community in which all are treated with respect and that uses problem solving (rather than rewards and punishments) to develop student responsibility and competence; and

• An approach to family participation involving home and schoolwide activities that are coordinated with the curriculum (Child Development Project 1993, p. 1).

A 1993 evaluation of the project reported:

> The results in San Ramon [the school district in which the program was initiated in 1982] demonstrated that the CDP program could be well-implemented in public elementary schools, and that it was effective in bringing about many of the positive effects for students that we had envisioned, relating to each of the three focal areas—social, ethical, and intellectual development (Child Development Project 1993, p. 3).

Another program reporting positive results is the Thomas Jefferson Center. An independent study of the Center's programs in the Los Angeles Schools "documented a 25 percent drop in major disciplinary problems; a 16 percent drop in student suspensions; an 18 percent drop in absenteeism; and a 40 percent drop in tardy students" (McCarthy 1992).

The effort to research evaluation of character education programs will help districts select or develop a program. For example, emerging research on the effects of comprehensive programs like the Child Development Project argue strongly on behalf of a broad approach. The credibility of the planning process will be enhanced if the evaluation and research component have been thoroughly examined early in the creation or selection of a program.

Lesson 3. Include an Implementation Assessment in the Evaluation Design.

Implementation assessment is often overlooked, and yet poor implementation of a program is frequently the cause of disappointing results. A careful assessment of the implementation process can reveal a variety of problems that can be corrected through mid-course adjustments. Some of these problems can be fatal to a program if untreated. Sometimes a vital component will have been omitted in the planning process. In other situations, staff development for some aspect of a program has been insufficient.

Many times a problem can be corrected through a modest adjustment in time or materials. If we had conducted a formal implementation assessment, we probably would have avoided some of the problems identified in the "Lessons Learned" portions of this book.

Lesson 4. Be Prepared to Answer Questions About Evaluating and Grading Individual Students.

· In the initial implementation stage of our program, a public debate over a proposed Pennsylvania department of education reform agenda occurred. Most of the debate centered on the OBE portion of the reform program. Parents feared that their children would be required to embrace "politically correct" positions on controversial topics. For example, through their reading of an early draft of the state's outcomes, some critics concluded that schools would be required to teach that "alternative lifestyles" were acceptable.

The implementation of a character education curriculum need not alter a school's current practice for evaluating and grading students. A character education curriculum, whether integrated or offered as a separate area, shares much with other disciplines. Evaluation approaches that work in those other disciplines will also serve character education.

For example, our elementary and junior high school Heartwood programs use evaluation strategies common to other literature-based curriculums. In the elementary schools, we evaluate students' understanding of a concept by having them describe the concept, generate examples of it through stories or other projects, or identify examples of it in and outside of school. We can do the same kind of evaluation with the Heartwood attributes.

At the secondary level, students write essays in English, social studies, and other subjects in which they often take a stand on a controversial topic. Their evaluations reflect the adequacy of supporting details, structure, logic, and mechanics, rather than the "political correctness" of their thesis. Those standards will also serve character education well.

The point that we make with parents is that their children will not be graded on the position they take with respect to a controversial topic. That is true of our current practice and will continue to be the case as we implement our character education curriculum.

Parents are equally concerned about our evaluation of moral acting or doing what is right. Again, I emphasize that current practice need not change. Before our character education initiative, our elementary report already included behaviors such as:

- Is courteous in speech and actions,
- Shows respect for others,
- Respects school property and the property of others,
- Observes rules and regulations.

Those standards will continue to be used as the district writes building-based prosocial behavior codes that reflect the core values. In these areas, there are "correct" positions that we expect students to take.

Lesson 5. Conduct Program Evaluations for Character Education.

Positive research or evaluation findings from other programs can go only so far in creating support for a district's character education effort. Eventually a district will need to report something about the results of its program. While experimental designs will be beyond the resources of many schools, correlational studies will not.

Assessment planning should begin with a review of the district's character education goals. For example, if a school seeks to promote respect and responsibility, staff members will need to determine which student behaviors they will examine. In brainstorming possibilities, a planning group might list items such as compliance with deadlines, the frequency with which students use the terms *respect* and *responsibility* in characterizing their own or another's behavior, or incidences of vandalism or theft.

Although anecdotes cannot be used to generalize about a program's effects, they can be useful in helping people understand its potential for positive outcomes. Let me offer an illustration. During October, one of our elementary schools was teaching *respect* as the Heartwood attribute of the month for the entire school. I observed two respect lessons in a 6th grade class. At the end of the lesson on the Friday before Halloween, the teacher pointed out that the class was concluding its discussion of respect. She asked the students what effect having read and discussed stories about respect would have on their behavior that Halloween weekend.

One student said that his elderly neighbor was frightened by the antics of some children and, consequently, she turned out her lights on Trick-or-Treat night. That, unfortunately, prompted some children to soap her windows and do other things such as turn over her porch furniture. He and a friend decided that they would reduce the time they spent trick-or-treating so they could take turns protecting her house from other children. Schools may want to include some anecdotal reports like this in their findings.

Having determined the student behaviors a school will examine in evaluating its character education program, the planners next need to determine how they will select the data. Some of the data will be relatively easy to collect and interpret because the information is quantifiable; for example, student suspensions for particular offenses, instances of tardiness, theft, or vandalism.

In addition to these possibilities, schools should not overlook the value of staff perceptions. For me, this was one of the most important indicators of the success of Heartwood in the first two Mt. Lebanon Schools to use the program. Uniformly, teachers reported changes such as improvement in the school's climate, especially increased respect being shown among students and and between students and staff. Further, they cited an increase in positive student behaviors, such as being more inclined to raise their hands and participate in class discussions.

Student self-reports represent another important form of data. Sometimes parents object to this practice because they worry about how the data will be used. To address this concern, planners should include parents in the development of the evaluation components. Everyone should be clear about how the information will be used to assess the program's effects, not individual students. To guard against the latter, students should not use their names in responding to surveys.

Computer technology allows schools to collect data from report cards and home notices without identifying individual students. A school may want to collect data related to some aspect of citizenship that is part of its reporting system. At the secondary level, one district uses a computerized system for reporting to parents between the times when report cards are issued. A frequent comment of these reports advises parents that a student needs to improve responsibility for completing work on time. A character education program seeking to nurture the development of responsible behavior could use the responsibility item from the home notice as baseline data.

Lesson 6. Involve Parents, Students, and All Staff in Developing Evaluation Components.

Involving parents in the early planning of the evaluation process will allow the staff to identify and understand parental concerns and questions that are a natural and desirable element of implementing character education programs. Parental concerns about evaluating and grading individual students are quite common in planning character education. Some parents will also express concern about surveys of student attitudes and behaviors. If an evaluation planning committee group can develop an evaluation scheme that is acceptable to the parent members of the committee, then the chances of acceptance by the larger parent community should be enhanced.

In addition to parents, representatives of all staff and students should be involved in the process of designing the evaluation components. Involving all reinforces the concept of a comprehensive program that seeks the active involvement of all employees and students. Custodians, for example, should have some voice in developing indicators of success. To illustrate, since Mt. Lebanon's core value of demonstrating active responsibility for the welfare of others includes the substatement "engaging in altruistic acts for impersonal others and the common good," a class might ask what this means in terms of the condition in which they leave the classroom for a night custodian whom they never see. A class's commitment to care for their classroom should produce results that the custodian can see and report.

Lesson 7. Establish Evaluation Partnerships with Colleges and Universities, Regional or County Support Units, or Other Agencies with Educational Missions.

Many school districts do not have an evaluation administrator or department or staff members with extensive preparation in the field of evaluation design. In many areas, regional or county support agencies such as an intermediate unit exist to provide support services that schools individually cannot afford. Schools should consider these agencies as an important resource in designing program and student evaluation processes.

Further, local colleges and universities that prepare teachers and administrators are often interested in developing research and evaluation partnerships with districts. Character education evaluations can be designed that serve to answer both the program questions of the school district and the research needs of college faculty or graduate students. The College at Cortland (SUNY), for example, has developed a questionnaire on academic attitudes and behaviors for its students that could be adapted for use at the secondary school level.

Another partnership source is an agency like a hospital or mental health organization that has an educational function. In Mt. Lebanon's case, a local hospital with an extensive drug and alcohol treatment program had the expertise necessary to assist in the design and implementation of an evaluation component for the character education parenting seminars. The hospital evaluators were especially helpful in the identification of success indicators.

Several organizations exist specifically for the purpose of assisting educators with their character education programs. The Josephson Institute, the Character Education Partnership, the ASCD Character Education Network, and the Ethics Resource Center are several that are listed in the Resources section. To illustrate the support available, the Josephson Institute offers a Values and Behavior Survey they will score and summarize for a modest fee. They offer national norms for comparison.

While careful evaluation designs can provide important information about the effects of character education, other important outcomes may fall outside the scope of an evaluation design for several reasons. First, some long-range goals cannot be measured during the time frame of a student's school experience. As a former English teacher, I always sought to encourage a lifelong love of reading in my students, even though I knew I would go to my grave generally ignorant of the results. Similarly, schools pursue the goal of good citizenship without knowing what percentage of their graduates regularly fulfill their obligation to vote.

Our work as educators in many instances reflects considerable hope and faith—hope that a goal will be achieved in the unknown future and faith that our experience and intuitions provide a reasonable basis for decision making when empirical data are not available. In no way am I trying to denigrate what research and evaluation can provide, but we must recognize that much of our work has a future orientation that does not lend itself to evaluations in the time frames available to us. I urge schools not to abandon goals just because they can't be measured during a student's school experience.

Second, character education will produce positive outcomes that extend beyond the stated goals of a program. Most of us can recall the positive influence that a teacher had on us. But such an influence may not be apparent to a close observer or even the student until many years later. My high school English teacher's ability to promote a love of literature and my math teacher's influence on my work ethic were not obvious to me until after I graduated.

A teacher who used the Heartwood curriculum told a story that described the potential of character education to influence people outside the scope of the program. At the beginning of the month, the teacher had sent home a letter informing parents that *honesty* would be the core attribute for that month's study. The letter identified the stories the teacher would be using and some of the activities designed to connect with the home.

Later in the month, on a Monday, a child presented the teacher with an excuse stating that she had been absent the previous Friday because she had been ill. Returning to school after lunch on that same day, the little girl was accompanied by her mother. The mother said that she couldn't live with the guilt of modeling dishonesty for her child. In the presence of her child, she admitted that the child's absence had been the result of the family's having taken a three-day weekend trip. Nurturing the core attributes in parents was not a goal of the school's Heartwood Program, but it was a positive outcome of it in this instance.

Much of our work as character educators is like farming: We plant seeds and do our best to promote their growth. Sometimes the seeds fall on fertile ground, sometimes they fall on rock, and sometimes they fall where we do not intend. Sometimes we find growth in surprising places.

A Final Observation

When we survey the conditions of our society, we can easily slip into a state of despair. As a teacher observed, some of our students come from homes where parents model values that contradict those we seek to develop in our schools. How can we expect students to develop the values of trust and honesty when they experience distrust and guile at home? Despite that reality, each of us has a sphere of influence, and that influence can make a positive difference in a child's life. If a school staff and representative community group can agree on a set of core values for a school to nurture, then that school will be an active character education partner with most families and will be a values oasis for students who don't encounter those values at home. Each of those situations offers the potential for positive outcomes. To turn our back on those possibilities is to reject Theodore Roosevelt's warning: "To educate a person in mind and not in morals is to educate a menace to society."

References

Albert, L. (1989). *A Teacher's Guide to Cooperative Discipline: How to Manage Your Classroom and Promote Self-Esteem.* Circle Pines, Minn.: American Guidance Service.

Baldwin, B. (1988). *Beyond the Cornucopia Kids: How to Raise Healthy Achieving Children.* Wilmington, N.C.: Direction Dynamics.

Bennett, W.J. (July 3, 1987). "Why Johnny Can't Abstain." *National Review,* p. 37.

Burns, J.M. (1978). *Leadership.* New York: Harper Torchbooks.

Buttram, J., J. Kruse, and J. Sidler. (July 1992). "Evaluation of the Heartwood Program: Final Report." Philadelphia: Research for Better Schools.

Coles, R. (1993). Keynote speech at the annual conference of the Association for Supervision and Curriculum Development, Washington, D.C.

Developmental Studies Center. (July 1993). "The Child Development Project: Description of Findings in Two Initial Districts and the First Phase of a Further Extension." Oakland, Calif.: Developmental Studies Center.

Elkind, D. (1981). *The Hurried Child: Growing Up Too Fast Too Soon.* Reading, Mass.: Addison Wesley.

Hanson, W. "Youth Leaders Choose Core Language for Character Education." *Ethics in Action.* Double Issue 19–20: 65–79. [Published by the Josephson Institute of Ethics.]

Hartshorne, H., and A. May. (1928–1930). *Studies in the Nature of Character: Vol. 1. Studies in Deceit; Vol. 2. Studies in Self Control; Vol. 3. Studies in the Organization of Character.* New York: Macmillan.

Jarns, T. (1990). Headmaster's Opening-of-School Address to Roxbury Latin School, Boston, Mass.

Josephson, M. (1992). *A Report: Ethics, Values, Attitudes and Behavior in American Schools.* Marina del Rey, Calif.: Josephson Institute of Ethics.

Kohlberg, L. (1984). *The Psychology of Moral Development: The Nature and Validity of Moral Stages.* New York: Harper and Row.

Leming, J.S. (November 1993). "In Search of Effective Character Education." *Educational Leadership* 51, 3: 63–71.

Lickona, T. (1983). *Raising Good Children: From Birth through the Teenage Years.* New York: Bantam.

Lickona, T. (1991). *Educating for Character: How Our Schools Can Teach Respect and Responsibility.* New York: Bantam.

Lickona, T. (November 1993). "Where Sex Education Went Wrong." *Educational Leadership* 51, 3: 84–89.

Lickona, T. (1994). Correspondence with Henry Huffman.

McCarthy, P.J. (1992). Letter from the Executive Vice President of the Thomas Jefferson Center.

Meade, J. (March 1990). "The Moral Life of America's School Children." *Teacher Magazine,* pp. 39–41.

Medved, M. (1992). *Hollywood vs. America: Popular Culture and the War on Traditional Values.* New York: HarperCollins.

Murphy, L., ed. (Winter 1988). "Portrait of the Child Development Project." In *Working Together,* No. 17. [Quarterly published by the Child Development Project, San Ramon, Calif.]

Nucci, L. P. (1989). "Challenging Conventional Wisdom about Morality: The Domain Approach to Values Education." In *Moral Development and Character Education: A Dialogue,* edited by L. Nucci. Berkeley, Calif.: McCutchan.

Peters, T.J., and R.H. Waterman Jr. (1982). *In Search of Excellence: Lessons from America's Best-Run Companies.* New York: Warner.

Piscolish, M. (1991). "Heartwood Program Pilot Year Evaluation: 1991 Summary Report." Pittsburgh: Pittsburgh Board of Public Education.

Postman, N. (1982). *The Disappearance of Childhood.* New York: Delacorte.

Saterlie, M.E. (October 1992). "The Baltimore County Model: Values Education in Public Schools." *Child and Adolescent Behavior Letter* (Brown University), p. 1.

Sollod, R.N. (March 18, 1992). "Point of View: The Hollow Curriculum." *The Chronicle of Higher Education* 38, 28: A60.

Turiel, E. (1983). *The Development of Social Knowledge: Morality and Convention.* Cambridge, Mass.: Cambridge University Press.

Vitz, P. (1986). *Censorship: Evidence of Bias in Our Children's Textbooks.* Ann Arbor, Mich.: Servant Books.

Watson, M., D. Solomon, V. Battistich, E. Schaps, and J. Solomon. (1989). "The Child Development Project: Combining Traditional and Developmental Approaches to Values Education." In *Moral Development and Character Education: A Dialogue,* edited by L. Nucci. Berkeley: McCutchan.

Willis, S. (1993). "Helping Students Resolve Conflict." *ASCD Update* 35, 10: 4–6.

Resources

Organizations

American Institute for Character Education. A nonprofit educational research foundation that offers a K–9 character education curriculum. Dimension II Building, 8918 Tesoro, Suite 220, San Antonio, TX 78217; Phone (512) 829-1727 or (800) 284-0499.

ASCD Character Education Network. Sponsored by ASCD and Boston University's Center for the Advancement of Ethics and Character, its mission is to help teachers and administrators struggling with the ethical and character formation aspect of their work. Kevin Ryan, Boston University, School of Education, 605 Commonwealth Avenue, Boston, MA 02215; Phone (617) 353-3262.

ASCD Conflict Resolution Network. Contact Mary Ellen Schaffer, Assistant Principal, Elsie Johnson School, 1380 Nautilus Lane, Hanover Park, IL 60613; Phone (708) 830-8770, Fax (708) 893-5452.

The Cambridge Group. The firm used by Mt. Lebanon School District to develop and implement its strategic plan. 5795 Carmichael Parkway, Montgomery AL 36117; Phone (205) 279-7150, Fax (205) 279-7151.

Center for the Advancement of Ethics and Character. Dedicated to helping schools recapture their role as moral educators, the Center has developed a model that emphasizes the curriculum as the primary vehicle for transmitting moral values to the young. The Center publicizes this model primarily through its "Teacher Academies" for elementary and secondary teachers and administrators. A similar program is directed toward college and university faculty responsible for the preparation of future teachers. The Center is also involved in researching and developing curricular materials for use by schools, teachers, and parents. Boston University, School of Education, 605 Commonwealth Ave., Boston, MA 02215; Phone (617) 343-3262.

Center for Character Education. An academic alliance of schools and universities bringing together educators interested in implementing a new model for moral education. The Integrated Character Education Model is based on the view that, in a person of mature character, knowledge, affect, and action are integrated. Duquesne University, School of Education, 410 Canevin Hall, Pittsburgh, PA 15282; Phone (412) 434-5191.

Center for the Fourth and Fifth Rs (Respect and Responsibility). Directed by Tom Lickona, this Center will sponsor an annual summer institute in character education (beginning in 1995), publish a *Fourth and Fifth Rs* newsletter, and help form a network of schools committed to teaching respect, responsibility, and related core values as the basis of good character. Education Department, SUNY Cortland, Cortland, NY 13045; Phone (607) 753-7881.

Center for Media Literacy. A nonprofit membership organization that translates media literacy research and theory into practical information, training, and educational tools for teachers, youth leaders, parents, and caregivers of children. Free catalog of teaching materials. 1962 S. Shenandoah St., Los Angeles, CA 90034; Phone (800) 226-94994, Fax (310) 559-2944.

The Character Counts Coalition. A project of the Josephson Institute; represents a national partnership of organizations and individuals involved in the education, training, or care of youth. Joined in a collaborative effort to improve the character of America's young people based on core ethical values, the Six Pillars of Character: Trustworthiness, Respect, Responsibility, Fairness, Caring, and Citizenship. Aims to combat violence, dishonesty, and irresponsibility by strengthening the moral fiber of the next generation. The Coalition will put the issue of character development on the forefront of the American agenda through a wide variety of grass-roots activities built on the conviction that character counts. 4640 Admiralty Way, Suite 1001, Marina del Rey, CA 90292; Phone (310) 306-1868.

The Character Education Institute of California University of Pennsylvania. A regional institute that provides character education support to school districts, higher education, businesses, and parents; facilitates research; and offers character education courses. Character Education Institute, California University of Pennsylvania, California, PA 15419-1394; Phone (412) 938-4000.

The Character Education Partnership. A nonpartisan coalition of organizations and individuals concerned about the moral crisis confronting America's youth and dedicated to developing moral character and civic virtue in our young people as a way of promoting a more compassionate and responsible society. Activities include a national clearinghouse, community programs, school support, publications, annual and regional forums, national awards and a media campaign. John A Martin, Executive Director, The Character Education Partnership, 1250 North Pitt Street, Alexandria, VA 22314; Phone (703) 739-9515, Fax (703) 739-4967.

The Child Development Project. An effort to take research knowledge and theory about how elementary-age schoolchildren learn and develop—intellectually, socially, and ethically—and translate it into a practical program for classroom, school, and home use. Its comprehensive approach to character education was a powerful influence in the creation of Mt.Lebanon's character education strategy. Developmental Studies Center, 2000 Embarcadero, Suite 305, Oakland, CA 94606-5300; Phone (510) 533-0213.

Communitarian Network. A coalition of individuals and organizations who have come together to shore up the moral, social, and political environment. This national organization is nonsectarian and nonpartisan. It sponsors an annual conference, produces position papers (on family, health-care reform, domestic disarmament, character and a civil society, and organ donation), and publishes a quarterly journal, *The Responsive Community: Rights and Responsibilities.* 2130 H Street, NW, #174, Washington, DC 20052; Phone (202) 994-7997, Fax (202) 994-1606.

Community Board Program. A conflict resolution resource. 1540 Market St., Suite 490, San Francisco, CA 94102; Phone (415) 552-1250, Fax (415) 626-0595.

Educators for Social Responsibility. School Conflict Resolution Programs, 23 Garden St., Cambridge, MA 02138; Phone (617) 492-1764.

Ethics Resource Center. Working to restore our society's ethical foundations by strengthening the capacity of our institutions to foster integrity, encourage ethical conduct, and support basic values. Since its establishment in 1977 as a nonprofit, nonpartisan, and nonsectarian educational organization, the Ethics Resource Center has developed practical and effective programs that address the evolving needs of the education, business, and government communities. Resources include research support, curricular materials, workshops, and conference sponsorship. 1120 G Street, NW, Washington, DC 20005; Phone (202) 737-2258.

Exploring Ethics Through Children's Literature. A literature-based ethics program for Grades 2–6. Critical Thinking Press & Software, P.O. Box 448, Dept. 4, Pacific Grove, CA 93950-0448; Phone (800) 458-4849, Fax (408) 372-3230.

The Heartwood Program. A multicultural, literature-based curriculum that uses classic children's stories from around the world to present universal values to children in grades K–8. Designed to foster moral literacy and ethical judgment by exposing students to seven core attributes: courage, loyalty, justice, respect, hope, honesty, and love. Mt. Lebanon uses this program in its elementary and junior high school programs.

The Heartwood Institute, 12300 Perry Highway, Wexford, PA 15090; Phone (412) 934-1777, Fax (412) 935-6888.

Institute on Media Education. A summer institute to help teachers and administrators to integrate media literacy into existing subject areas; to develop new teaching methods that help students think critically about what they see, read, and watch; to analyze newspapers and television news and examine press influence on the coverage of the American political process; and to implement media awareness outreach programs in their schools and communities. Programs in Professional Education, 339E Gutman Library, Harvard Graduate School of Education, Cambridge, Mass. 02138; Phone (617) 495-3572, Fax (617) 496-8051.

The Joseph and Edna Josephson Institute of Ethics. A nonprofit educational and leadership training organization seeking to increase the nation's awareness of ethical issues and to provide individuals with the skills to make their behaviors more ethical. Activities include research, publications, and skills training workshops; also sponsors the Character Education Coalition. Josephson Institute, 4640 Admiralty Way, Suite 1001, Marina del Ray, CA 90292; Phone (310) 306-1868, Fax (310) 827-1864.

National Association for Mediation in Education (NAME). A conflict resolution resource. 205 Hampshire House, Box 33635, Amherst, MA 01003-3635; Phone (413) 545-2462.

Parent & Child Guidance Center. The mental health agency that delivers the character education parenting series. 2644 Banksville Road, Pittsburgh, PA 15216; Phone (412) 343-5698, Fax (412) 343-8249.

Personal Responsibility Education Program (PREP). A school-business-community partnership representing 22 public school districts that is designed to develop student character, personal responsibility, and achievement. The Network for Educational Development, 13157 Olive Spur Road, St. Louis, MO 63141; Phone (314) 576-3535, ext. 130, Fax (314) 576-4996.

St. Francis Health System. The agency that conducted evaluations of the character education parenting programs the school district sponsored through a local mental health agency. The Center for Chemical Dependency Treatment, 400 45th Street, Pittsburgh, PA 15201-1198; Phone (412) 622-4511.

The Jefferson Center for Character Education. Formed in 1963 for the purpose of publishing and promoting programs for schools that teach sound character values and personal responsibility; 202 South Lake Ave., #240, Pasadena, CA 91101; Phone (818) 792-8130.

Publications

Amundson, K. (1991). *Teaching Values and Ethics: Problems and Solutions.* Arlington, Va.: American Association of School Administrators.

Bennett, W.J., ed. (1993). *The Book of Virtues: A Treasury of Great Moral Stories.* New York: Simon & Schuster.

Benninga, J.S., ed. (1991). *Moral, Character, and Civic Education in the Elementary School.* New York: Teachers College Press.

Coles, R. (1989). *The Call of Stories: Teaching and the Moral Imagination.* Boston: Houghton Mifflin.

Coles, R. (1990). *The Spiritual Life of Children.* Boston: Houghton Mifflin.

Damon, W. (1992). *Some Do Care: Contemporary Lives of Moral Commitment.* New York: Free Press.

Etzioni, A. (1993). *The Spirit of Community.* New York: Crown.

Goodlad, J.I., R. Soder, and K. Sirotnik, eds. (1990). *The Moral Dimensions of Teaching.* San Francisco: Jossey-Bass.

Harmin, M. 1990). *How to Plan a Program for Moral Education.* Alexandria, Va.: Association for Supervision and Curriculum Development.

Hill, P.T., G.E. Foster, and T. Gendler.(1990). *High Schools with Character.* Santa Monica, Calif.: The Rand Corporation.

Jackson, P.R., R. Boostrom, D. Hansen. (1993). *The Moral Life of Schools.* San Francisco: Jossey-Bass.

Kubey, R., and M. Csikszentmihalyi. (1990). *Television and the Quality of Life: How Viewing Shapes Everyday Experience.* Hillsdale, N.J.: Lawrence Erlbaum Associates.

National School Boards Association. (1987). *Building Character in the Public Schools.* Alexandria, Va.: National School Boards Association.

Piaget, J. (1932). *The Moral Development of the Child.* London: Routledge and Kegan Paul.

Raths, L.E., M. Harmin, and S. Sidney. (1966). *Values and Teaching.* Columbus, Ohio: Charles E. Merrill.

Shea, G.F. (1988). *Practical Ethics.* New York: American Management Association.

Sizer, N.F. (1984). *Making Decisions: Cases for Moral Discussion.* Boston: The Independent School Press.

Strike, K., E.J. Haller, and J.F. Soltis. (1988). *The Ethics of School Administration.* New York: Teachers College Press.

Wilson, J. Q. (1993). *The Moral Sense.* New York: The Free Press.

Wynne, E.A., and K. Ryan. (1992). *Reclaiming Our Schools: A Handbook on Teaching Character, Academics, and Discipline.* New York: Merrill.